THE AMERICAN DOCTRINE

THE AMERICAN DOCTRINE
(REFLECTIONS FOR BEGINNERS)
by

Dario Lisiero

Copyright © 2008 by Dario Lisiero

All rights reserved. No part of this book may be reproduced, stored, or transmitted by any means—whether auditory, graphic, mechanical, or electronic—without written permission of both publisher and author, except in the case of brief excerpts used in critical articles and reviews. Unauthorized reproduction of any part of this work is illegal and is punishable by law.

Library of Congress Control Number 2008906451

ISBN 978-0-6152-3851-7

CONTENTS

Foreword   ix

First Part: Presentation of "The American Doctrine"

Introduction	3
The Monroe Doctrine	5
The Roosevelt Corollary	9
The Lodge Corollary	13
The Truman Doctrine	15
The Eisenhower Doctrine	19
The Domino Theory	21
The Kennedy Doctrine	23
The Johnson Doctrine	29
The Nixon Doctrine	31
The Carter Doctrine	37
The Reagan Doctrine	43
The Weinberger Doctrine	51
The Clinton Doctrine	57
The Bush Doctrine	65
Conclusion	73
Definition of Doctrine	77
Division of Doctrines	79

Can a Doctrine Change?	80
The Catholic Doctrine	81
The American Doctrine	82

Second Part: Documentation for "The American Doctrine"

The Monroe Doctrine	87
Theodore Roosevelt's Corollary to the Monroe Doctrine	91
Foreign Policy	91
Arbitration Treaties—Second Hague Conference	94
Policy Toward Other Nations of the Western Hemisphere	94
Henry Cabot Lodge: Corollary to the Monroe Doctrine	97
Truman Doctrine	101
President Nixon's Speech on *Vietnamization*	109
Jimmy Carter, State of the Union Address 1980	119
Ronald Reagan	129
Ronald Reagan	131
Casper W. Weinberger "The Uses of Military Power"	143
Remarks by President Bill Clinton on Foreign Policy	155
Rebuilding America's Defenses: Strategy, Forces, and Resources for a New Century	173
Introduction	173
Key Findings	178
I -Why Another Defense Review?	180
II -Four Essential Missions	186
Project Participants	201
U.S. Interventions in Latin America	203

Where to Go for More Information	**219**
Other Publications by Dario Lisiero	**221**

FOREWORD

In an election year that is so pivotal in the lives of every American and so crucial for billions of human beings around the world, you would expect to hear from both the media and the presidential candidates some reference to the *American Doctrine*. Yet surprisingly, no one is mentioning this highly sensitive subject.

The airwaves, newspapers, magazines, and other instruments of communication may be full of information on issues and programs (and on the lives, virtues, and vices of the Democratic and Republican candidates), but there's no mention of the American Doctrine. Even when the partisan candidates battle fiercely for supremacy by touching on the most diverse of problems, we still won't find any reference to the American Doctrine—instead, all will be fighting tooth and nail to place themselves in the center of the political spectrum, thus avoiding any extremism or appearance of impropriety.

The truth is that everyone wants to appear deeply religious and God-fearing while not mentioning Him often, even ignoring Him publicly. All candidates want to portray themselves as antiracist and pro-equality. Nobody dares to be against equal opportunities or minorities.

Everybody wants to improve the economy, the health care system, and the environment. Everybody is more than eager to take on our enemies, defeat terrorism, and bring home the troops.

However, nobody seems anxious or impatient to unveil his or her political doctrine and promote a debate on what America is, what America should be, and how America should be viewed and portrayed abroad. But rest assured, as soon as whoever is elected is faced with the need for military action, he will not hesitate to put forward a fancy political doctrine that explains and justifies even the most unexplainable and unjustifiable act.

We dare to ask: Why is political doctrine greatly absent in the presidential campaign? What is the reason behind this unexplainable vacuum, this awkward conspiracy of silence?

No answers are forthcoming for these provocative questions. Probably behind this beautiful smoke and mirrors' presentation by our prepacked and highly palatable candidates lurks a great fear and an understandable reluctance to go onto controversial and slippery terrain. They believe it is better to circumscribe speeches and debates within the parameters of familiar pastures than to overstep the boundaries of normalcy and jump into the unknown.

Not all of us are politicians, prophets, or experts on any esoteric political science theory. However, we are free to write and make our voices heard. For this simple reason, as an ordinary citizen concerned with the future of our country, I as the author would like to venture beyond slogans, stereotypes, party lines, media propaganda, popular misconceptions, and ideological deformations to discover what America has to offer in the realm of political doctrine. The presentation of every doctrine will be as impartial and dispassionate as humanly possible.

This book is divided into two distinct parts. The first contains "The American Doctrine" with the "Reflections for Beginners," while the second part, "Documentation for the American Doctrine," contains the original documents, speeches, etc. that reflect the American doctrine of the historical figures presented in the first part. That way, if you as the reader don't agree with or share my views, you can always examine the historical documents and draw your own conclusions.

As the same painting or sculpture can inspire people differently, a political figure can appeal to one person while leaving another unmoved. Points of view are just that: points of view. Nobody can claim to capture the whole personality of a public figure or to be the sole interpreter of his or her philosophy.

Keep this in mind: these reflections are a partial tool of interpretation with no pretense of being comprehensive, exclusive, or even right.

FIRST PART

PRESENTATION OF "THE AMERICAN DOCTRINE"

INTRODUCTION

In our fast-moving and rapidly changing society, nothing is written in stone. Sacred values and noble traditions are being transformed before our eyes.

The same fate seems to befall words that had remained immutable for centuries. Undoubtedly, one of these words is *doctrine*. Most of us at one time or another have come across the expression "the Monroe doctrine" or "the Bush doctrine," but probably few of us have tried to conduct a thorough investigation into this unusual subject.

I must confess that the word *doctrine* in conjunction with a name of an American president has always intrigued me. The mere sound of it has never failed to arouse my curiosity, raising in the process many disparate questions. How many doctrines are there? Do they have the same origin and definition? Alternatively, do they differ radically from one another? Who has the authority to proclaim a doctrine? Once declared, is it binding?

These and many other questions propelled me on a frantic search for the meaning and definition of that awesome word. I was perfectly aware of two major areas where this word is commonly used: religious and political. I was familiar with religious doctrines, but not with political ones. Hence, in my fervor, I start a journey of discovery into the most eloquent and insightful exponents of the American doctrine.

After venturing into this astonishing and eye-opening territory, it will be useful to formulate a definition of *political doctrine* that clearly distinguishes it from other religious and secular doctrines. Some other considerations regarding the characteristics of specific doctrines will be used to complement the picture.

1
THE MONROE DOCTRINE

(March 4, 1817–March 4, 1825)[1]

Without any further delay, let us get acquainted with the Monroe doctrine, the root and origin of all other American political doctrines. The American doctrine has its genesis in two principles enunciated by President James Monroe on December 2, 1823.[2]

The *first principle* stated that the "American Continents, by the free and independent condition which they have assumed and maintain, are henceforth not to be considered as subjects for further colonization by any European Power."

The *second principle* implied that Monroe backed the new independence by the Latin America republics. As the American and European political systems were "essentially different," Monroe made it quite clear that the United States would consider any effort by European nations "to extend their system to any portion of this hemisphere as dangerous to our peace and safety." In this message,

---

[1] All the historical information found in this first part comes from Wikipedia, the free Internet encyclopedia.
See also Foreign policy of the United States in Answers.com
[2] See The Monroe Doctrine in Answers.com.
See also Part Two, document 1, The Monroe Doctrine.

Monroe is adamantly asserting that the American continents have reached adulthood. After coming of age, they do not need any tutelage or interference whatsoever. Moreover, the United States is asserting itself to be the oldest brother of the two new continents, the one in charge of keeping an eye and defending its other American siblings from any foreign intervention.

However, even if Monroe's message was perfectly clear in its twofold content, its rise to prominence took an awfully long time. In the American conscience, it remained dormant for a period of roughly two decades. The first president who resurrected it as a form of policy justification was James K. Polk in the 1840s.

On the international scene, the Monroe message did not receive any foreign acknowledgment. What is worse, it was totally disregarded during the entire nineteenth century while the European powers meddled at their discretion in affairs of the American continents. Yet in spite of its humble beginnings, this most astonishing piece of American foreign policy remains a Magna Carta for the Americas and the seed that would produce a new global superpower. As was true with the Magna Carta, in which the King of England had to give up some privileges in favor of his subjects, in the Monroe Doctrine, the European nations in particular and all nations in general were told to give up their colonialist pretensions and their urges to intervene in the affairs of this entire hemisphere.

Regardless of its relevance in the American conscience, the Monroe Doctrine never became international law and never was accepted as normative. On the contrary, it was purposely trampled on by the colonialist powers, and even rejected with resentment and hatred by the Latin American nations.[3]

This notwithstanding, the United States never backed off from its convictions and assertions. The more the military muscles and economic power of the United States grew, the bigger the U.S. sphere of influence became and the more solid and established the Monroe Doctrine turned out to be. Only the decline of the American might could subtract significance, applicability, or effectiveness from this fundamental piece of the American credo.

---

[3] See Part Two (last document), U.S Interventions in Latin America. www.**zo**mpist.com/latam.html

Whether this tenet is philosophically, morally, or even politically acceptable is totally irrelevant. Historically, this is the way it is, and nothing in the world will ever change it. For example, the law of gravity can be discussed, argued, ignored, accepted, or even rejected, but the reality of gravity will never change. In the same way, the Monroe Doctrine can be exalted or vituperated, ignored or proclaimed from the rooftops, but it will remain the same, unscathed and unharmed.

Not only physical reality but human relations are affected by gravitational poles. We dare to ask: Are total neutrality and isolationism, complete liberty and democracy, absolute sovereignty and independence merely empty words? Will we always be confronted with the crude reality of dominance and dependence, mastery and slavery, imposition and submission? The ways nations relate to each other can be made more genteel and less brutal and barbarian. But as these negativities would seem to be in the nature of things, can they ever be eliminated? In particular, is this state of dominance and dependence spelled out unambiguously in any subsequent American doctrine?

2
THE ROOSEVELT COROLLARY

(September 14, 1901–March 3, 1909)

Almost a century passed before any innovation to the Monroe Doctrine was introduced. It was prompted by significant changes in the hemisphere at the very beginning of the twentieth century. The strangling economic ties of some Central and South American countries that were unable to repay their debts to powerful European lenders were seriously jeopardizing the stability of the continent. The United States resented this mounting interference of European nations in the internal affairs of Latin American countries and recognized an urgent need to add a corollary to the Monroe Doctrine.

In 1902, President Theodore Roosevelt was appalled by the blockade and bombardment of Venezuela by Germany and Great Britain. In May 1904, he wrote a public letter to his secretary of war reminding him of his duties of intervention. Finally, in December of the same year, in his message to the Congress,[4] he made clear his intention that any meddling of foreign powers in the American continents would no longer be tolerated:

---

[4] See Part Two, document 2, Theodore Roosevelt's Corollary to the Monroe Doctrine.

All that this country desires is to see the neighboring countries stable, orderly, and prosperous. Any country whose people conduct themselves well can count upon our hearty friendship. If a nation shows that it knows how to act with reasonable efficiency and decency in social and political matters, if it keeps order and pays its obligations, it need fear no interference from the United States. Chronic wrongdoing, or an impotence which results in a general loosening of the ties of civilized society, may in America, as elsewhere, ultimately require intervention by some civilized nation, and in the Western Hemisphere the adherence of the United States to the Monroe Doctrine may force the United States, however reluctantly, in flagrant cases of such wrongdoing or impotence, to the exercise of an international police power.

This is the *Roosevelt Corollary* to the Monroe Doctrine, which establishes a policing role for the United States. It states that America has an ingrained and congenital duty to make sure that every nation in this hemisphere behaves in a civilized manner, running its affairs efficiently, keeping order within its borders, and paying its obligations.

What was implicit in the Monroe Doctrine regarding a supervisory American role in the rest of the two continents was made explicit in the Roosevelt Corollary, but with a substantial difference. It appears in the Monroe Doctrine that the supervisory role by the United States would be exercised in a "brotherly" manner, but the Roosevelt Corollary clearly has the United States carrying it out using police powers and methods. Instead of *persuasion* such as a brother would use with his siblings, the United States would be using *pure coercion*, in the way a police state conducts itself in the event of a riot.

It was obvious that America was aware of its new position of strength and influence. Its words were not empty threats or mere intimidating tactics. Those soft words were carrying a big stick, capable of making a military strike anywhere on the South American continent and requiring any rebellious Latin American country to immediately comply with U.S. demands.

From this growing military might, the Roosevelt Corollary was deriving its strength and validity. Without it, the Corollary would have been meaningless and ineffective.

However, the countries affected by this new policy neither looked benevolently upon their big brother in the North nor accepted his intromission in their internal affairs. Resentment and hostility would mark their relations, sometimes reaching the boiling point of outright hatred.

3
THE LODGE COROLLARY

(Senator Henry Cabot Lodge:
May 12, 1850–November 9, 1924)

A few years later in 1912, Senator Henry Cabot Lodge introduced a new corollary[5] to the Monroe Doctrine, which was approved by the Senate. It read:

> Resolved, that when any harbor or other place in the American continents is so situated that the occupation thereof for naval or military purposes might threaten the communications or the safety of the United States, the government of the United States could not see without grave concern the possession of such harbor or other place by any corporation or association which has such a relation to another government, not American, as to give that government practical power of control for national purposes. . . .

The Lodge Corollary was a reaction to a Japanese syndicate's move to purchase from Mexico a considerable portion of Baja California

---

[5] See Part Two, document 3 – The Lodge Corollary.

including Magdalena Bay, a harbor of strategic value. America was extremely sensitive to any acquisition of American land by a foreign power or corporation. However, after the U.S. Senate ratified the Lodge Corollary, the Japanese government denied any connection to the syndicate, and an agreement for the purchase was never reached.

Whatever the intentions of the Japanese business group, the United States, in line with the spirit of the Monroe Doctrine, had added another corollary to it with the clear purpose of keeping any foreign power from setting its foot permanently on the continent. The United States was the *supreme guardian* of the hemisphere, keeping its eyes peeled to spot any potential intruders.

4
THE TRUMAN DOCTRINE

(April 12, 1945–January 20, 1953)

After World War II, the international scene changed completely. Despite defeating the Nazis and their Axis allies, a new and powerful enemy now threatened world peace and stability.

The "Red Scare" or "Communist Scare" was a frightening political phenomenon very difficult to understand unless you experienced it. All of a sudden, the military machine of Russia and its irresistible Marxist ideology seemed to take over the entire democratic world. Strong and combative communist parties were mushrooming in the bosom of the most stable occidental democracies.

However, although facing internal enemies (communist Americans and their sympathizers) and external foes (Russian military divisions), the United States rose to the challenge. The answer was clear and unequivocal: total elimination of any trace of communism on American soil (McCarthyism) and total containment of any Russian expansion along the "northern tier" of the Mediterranean first, and elsewhere second (the Truman Doctrine). From then on, evil (Russia) and good (America) would be locked in a mortal combat throughout the entire Cold War era. Nothing was more frightening than this historical period during which the nuclear threat was like the Sword of Damocles hanging by a single horsehair over humankind. Any misstep, any miscalculation, any imprudence could have caused the immediate obliteration of our civilization.

For the moment, I will leave aside McCarthyism to focus on the Truman doctrine of containment. In 1947, the Soviet Union seemed to be seeking access to the Persian Gulf, the Mediterranean, and the entire Middle East. The Truman administration believed a Soviet hegemony in this oil-rich region would provoke the demise of Western Europe and ultimately threaten America.

After World War II, the United States was perceived in a different light. It was the ultimate ally and the supreme liberator for any nation at risk. At this particular juncture in history, the ugly image of Yankee imperialism was totally absent from the European and world conscience. Instead a sense of gratitude and admiration was surfacing everywhere for the job well done in liberating Europe from the Nazi oppression.

As President Truman was well in tune with this positive perception of his country, and most of all confident in his military superiority, he was listening with sympathetic ears to Greece's pleas for help. Turkey too was in imminent danger of being swallowed up in the Russian expansionist push. The crisis in the Mediterranean clearly became a problem when the British government declared itself financially incapable of maintaining its long-standing commitments in that region. The combination of all these historical circumstances resulted in the Truman Doctrine.

Before a joint session of Congress on March 12, 1947,[6] the president described with vigor the dangers in Greece and Turkey and unequivocally laid out his doctrine. This can be summed up in one simple sentence: "I believe that it must be the policy of the United States to support free peoples who are resisting attempted subjugation by armed minorities or by outside pressures." Here "outside pressures" is a clear reference to the Russian threat while the "armed minorities" are communist movements inside the country.

The military and economic support offered by Truman to Greece and Turkey was met with widespread opposition within Congress and by the president's critics. This notwithstanding, the aid program of $400 million was approved. This saved the two nations from certain

---

[6] See Part Two, document 4 – The Truman Doctrine.

invasion by the Soviet Union and lent great credibility to the theory of containment.

By reading carefully Truman's address to the Congress, it is possible to discover a few components that constitute the quintessence of the true American soul. Although I am no expert on the subject and hold no illusion of being exhaustive, here are some thoughts regarding the most relevant elements.

First, the president had a picture-perfect analysis of the situation. Greece and Turkey were in dire need of external help. The Soviet Union was threatening their existence as free countries. Neither the United Nations nor other individual nations could offer measurable aid to avoid catastrophe. Only the United States had the necessary means to provide the requested assistance.

Second, there was an unequivocal cry for help coming from those countries. America in good conscience couldn't disregard this plea, because not only was one nation's freedom in imminent danger, but the stability of the entire region, thus putting U.S. safety and survival at risk. As nobody else could help at this point in time, America had the moral obligation to respond to those cries for assistance.

President Truman had identified a real enemy, the Soviet Union, which was intrinsically evil because of its totalitarian regime and its total suppression of all liberties. Finally, he wasn't acting unilaterally, ignoring either the United Nations or Congress.

In general, America could not be impotent and powerless, such as Europe, or attend the funeral of its highest political ideals along with freedom and democracy. To do so would be an historical mistake of unforeseeable consequences.

This is the true American Spirit, aware of the external dangers, respectful of the international community, and sympathetic to any freedom-loving nation. It did not reflect any imposition of its will, unilateralism, or arrogance that would be contrary to the spirit and values it was preaching and defending. Freedom must be saved with freedom, as to do the opposite would be a mockery of U.S. principles and a slap in the face to democracy.

For these reasons, the Truman Doctrine is considered an amazing monument to all that is great and good in this country. Never before or after (except for President Carter) has America reached the pinnacle of world opinion to be seen as the true cradle of democracy and believable defender of freedom.

5
THE EISENHOWER DOCTRINE

(January 20, 1953–January 20, 1961)

When President Dwight D. Eisenhower faced the same Communist threat as his predecessor Truman, he didn't create a new doctrine. Instead, he expanded on the previous president's position by stressing the *doctrine of containment* and the *domino theory*.

With regards to the doctrine of containment, in 1956 after the Suez Crisis, Eisenhower reminded America of the spread of "international communism". On January 5, 1957, he told Congress that he regarded "as vital to the national interest and world peace the preservation of the independence and integrity of the nations of the Middle East." Furthermore, he would assist any "nation or group of nations in the general area of the Middle East desiring such assistance" in order to preserve their independence.

In 1958 during the Lebanon Crisis, Lebanese president Camille Chaumon asked the United States for immediate military assistance to oppose attempts by Syria and Egypt to destabilize his government. In spite of considerable Congressional opposition, Eisenhower deployed the Sixth Fleet and landed a contingent of fifteen thousand troops in Lebanon. In this manner he ensured that Lebanon could freely elect its own president.

Eisenhower's policy made America and the world aware that the United States had clearly assumed a new global role in the preservation of regional stability and promotion of its own national interests. This new awareness, with the consequent new foreign policy stand of the United States being the world's "watchdog," would have different effects as to America and the rest of the world. However, Eisenhower's foreign policy did not represent any real departure from the Truman Doctrine—only a new perception of America's involvement overseas.

6
THE DOMINO THEORY

The domino theory is premised on the idea that one event will put in motion a train of similar events. In our case, if a nation falls under communist control, the neighboring nations will suffer the same fate. This theory originated during the Hitler era. Although mentioned by President Truman, it became prevalent and widespread with Eisenhower.

The idea stemmed from a pre–World War II event. In 1938 at the Munich Conference, Britain and France allowed Hitler to take a part of Czechoslovakia. Many thought this to be a monumental mistake. At that point, Hitler could have been stopped without difficulty. Instead in a very short period, a "domino effect" occurred in which Poland was invaded and partitioned while Denmark and Norway were overrun. Luxembourg, the Netherlands, Belgium, and France followed with the whole of Europe being threatened.

From the ashes of World War II, Joseph Stalin of Russia emerged as a ruthless dictator and a mass murderer, with a voracious appetite. The acquisition of the atomic bomb in 1949 made him a bigger threat than Hitler had been.

As Truman's undersecretary of state, Dean Acheson played a significant role in formulating both the Truman Doctrine and the European Recovery Program. In 1947, he persuaded U.S. congressional leaders to support aid measures for Greece. On this occasion, he provided this illustration:

> I knew we were met at Armageddon....Like apples in a barrel infected by one rotten one, the corruption of Greece would infect Iran and all to the east. It would also carry infection to Africa through Asia Minor and Egypt, and to Europe through Italy and France, already threatened by the strongest domestic communist parties in Western Europe.

This way of thinking became prevalent during the Eisenhower presidency. His new secretary of state, John Foster Dallas, pushed a very radical version of the domino theory for all East Asia.

Although the Vietnam War at first seemed to validate the theory, it eventually revealed its feet of clay. However, this "domino" mentality remained imbedded in the American psyche for a very long time, justifying military interventions and CIA covert operations.

7

THE KENNEDY DOCTRINE

(January 20, 1961–November 22, 1963)

John F. Kennedy, the man who captured the imagination of countless people at home and abroad, was a hopeful visionary of a new bright future. Along with other world leaders such as Pope John XXIII (1958–1963) and Nikita Sergeyevich Khrushchev (1958–1964), Kennedy raised the level of expectations to new heights.

At that time, a second Renaissance in politics, religion, and economics seemed around the corner. A new Camelot mentality, in which the noblest ideals on earth were being pursued, was gaining a foothold on our troubled planet. The full meaning of the Kennedy Doctrine can only be discerned within this framework of hope, renovation, and incredible expectations.

The Kennedy Doctrine addresses two main concerns: the containment of communism and the improvement of human conditions. In Kennedy's mind, these two actions were so inextricably connected that by implementing one, the other would inevitably be fostered. Thus the two missions would go hand in hand and it would be naïve of anyone to think the opposite.

Accordingly, Kennedy called upon the public at large to assist in "a struggle against the common enemies of man: tyranny, poverty, disease and the war itself." This concise phrase reveals Kennedy's mentality, vision, and dream. A moral imperative touches everyone's conscience and unites all men of goodwill in the struggle against the plagues of our society that must be fought against courageously and decisively.

However, this unusual call to action contained inherent contradictions. Obviously, the struggle against poverty and disease does not need any military force. However, when it comes to tyranny and war, is that still feasible? If not, how can war be eliminated by using war? Isn't it a vicious circle to try to eradicate tyranny and war by adopting the same dynamics?

Kennedy was probably aware of this untenable position on a philosophical basis. However, as he was offering more a vision and a dream, he didn't seem to mind contradictions and incongruities.

However, when the time of practical decisions came, Kennedy had to struggle to overcome his internal demons. Not always would he be able to be faithful to his ideals of a peaceful development to save humankind.

The containment of communism is clearly an extension and reaffirmation of the previous doctrines. In his January 20, 1961, inaugural address, Kennedy warned the world, and in particular the Soviet Union:

> Let every nation know, whether it wishes us well or ill, that we shall pay any price, bear any burden, meet any hardship, support any friend, oppose any foe, in order to assure the survival and the success of liberty.

There should be no doubt that the president of the United States was determined to use military force wherever liberty is being suppressed. But would these extraordinary words in fact be accompanied by a big stick?

The second part of Kennedy's vision, the improvement of human conditions, offers a plan of closer collaboration with Latin American governments. He called it the *Alliance for Progress*, saying:

> I have called on all the people of the hemisphere to join in a new Alliance for Progress—*Alianza para el Progreso*—a vast cooperative effort, unparalleled in magnitude and nobility of

purpose, to satisfy the basic needs of the American people for homes, work and land, health and schools—*techo, trabajo y tierra, salud y escuela.*

To achieve this goal political freedom must accompany material progress. Our Alliance for Progress is an alliance of free governments –and it must work to eliminate tyranny from a hemisphere in which it has no rightful place. Therefore let us express our special friendship to the people of Cuba and the Dominican Republic—and the hope they will soon rejoin the society of free men, uniting with us in our common effort.

More than a doctrine, Kennedy was putting forward a hopeful vision for a better future in Latin America. If the United States helped in improving basic human conditions, the specter of tyranny and oppression could be avoided, and the subjugated people of Cuba and the Dominican Republic would be able to return to the fold of democracy and freedom.

However, close partnership and collaboration were necessary to achieve this coveted goal. To the brethren in the hemisphere, Kennedy talked in a fraternal way. He didn't threaten them with any stick or military force, but only gave them a brotherly helping hand, as it should be. Help and persuasion goes a long way in solving conflicts and maintaining peace and stability. This attitude was a clear departure from the previous postures that involved superimposed policing methods and from future activities that would include active destabilizations and the overthrowing of left-wing leaders.

However, the ambivalence and contradictions in Kennedy's position appeared clearly in the situation that resulted in the Bay of Pigs invasion. On the one hand, Kennedy had planned to overthrow the Castro regime by using an armed brigade of Cuban exiles. On the other hand, he had made every effort to hide his government's connection to the projected invasion. In fact, Kennedy, in upholding plausible deniability, changed the landing site and cancelled the air strikes at the last moment. These two critical decisions meant U.S air cover and support was lacking during the invasion, thus sealing its fate.

Quite different was Kennedy's stand on the Cuban missile crisis. The Soviet Union was meddling dangerously in the Latin American continent. Kennedy's resolve to oppose any foreign interference even if meant resorting to nuclear weapons was unmistakable and unshakable.

This contradictory attitude finds its final explanation in his utopian vision and Camelot mentality. To use military force against Cuba or elsewhere in the hemisphere would have been contrary to the spirit of the Alliance for Progress. However, military intervention to crush the Cuban revolution would have been in total accordance with the basic principal of containment of communism. In spite of this contradictory ideology, what prevailed in Kennedy was his vision of progress and transformation without violence. In this light, many of his ambiguous decisions can be explained or at least partially understood. Kennedy, the charismatic leader of the free world, was a prisoner and victim of his own dream and vision.

Finally, a brief overview of Kennedy's perceived role on the world stage may be helpful. What is interesting now is not a regional but a global view of his overall mission. According to the testimony of William Averell Harriman, a man who served in several posts in the administration, "President Kennedy was the first President that I know of, who was really his own secretary of state. He dealt with every aspect of foreign policy, and he knew about everything that was going on."[7]

Kennedy was also a real commander in chief and the man in charge. In his inaugural address, this visionary man saw clearly his position in the international system. He firmly believed that the United States had both the power and ability to control events on a global scale—and it should do so. "In the long history of the world only a few generations have been granted the role of defending freedom from its hour of maximum danger. I do not shrink from this responsibility—I welcome it."

Here too, this awesome role of defender and protector of the free world is seen primarily in the light of disarmament and global cooperation rather than military intervention. Kennedy was ready to use the sword only as a last resort. His interventions in international hot spots (Greece, Turkey, and mainly in Vietnam) were basically restricted to economic assistance and technical expertise.

---

[7] Wikipedia. See Kennedy Doctrine, Answers.com

Deep dawn, Kennedy was not a warmonger, but a motivational and pacifist inspirator. His charismatic figure was larger than life. His influence transcended temporal and geographic barriers. More than a doctrine, Kennedy offered a breath of fresh air, a new spirit in international politics, and a hopeful vision of a brighter future for humankind.

For these reason, on the canvas of this visionary man there is room for inaccuracies, contradictions, and paradoxes. War can coexist with alliances and cooperation or military interventions with a helping hand. Sticks and carrots can find a perfect symbiosis in Kennedy without diminishing his stature; on the contrary, these contrasting symbols made him one of the greatest politicians of the twentieth century.

8
THE JOHNSON DOCTRINE

(November .22, 1963–January 20, 1969)

On November 22, 1963, an hour and thirty-nine minutes after the brutal assassination of President Kennedy, Lyndon B. Johnson was sworn in aboard Air Force One. If it would be difficult for anyone to fill Kennedy's shoes, this was particularly true for his vice-president as their styles and personalities could not have been more at odds. The strong and genuine man from Texas couldn't compete with the refined and sophisticated man from Massachusetts.

Kennedy was beyond doctrine, while Johnson was short of it. Kennedy had a spirit and a vision, while Johnson had a few basic beliefs.

Johnson doctrine, if we dare call it so, was sustained and guided by two convictions acquired during his political career: the domino theory and the containment of communism, which were interchangeable and could have been reduced to one principle: *communism is evil and must be stopped anywhere and at any cost.*

The advance of communism in the Far East and particularly in Vietnam put Johnson's belief in the domino theory to the test. The more the communists were making progress in that region, the more Johnson believed in the domino effect of one nation falling after the other. He feared that if it were not stopped, communism would spread through the Pacific, first taking over the Hawaiian Islands, then inevitably reaching the American West Coast, and finally swallowing up San Francisco and the whole state of California.

Accordingly, Johnson felt a need to stop that evil by military force at its very source. The technical assistance and the expertise offered by the Kennedy Administration to South Vietnam was nothing compared to the military involvement of President Johnson. However, soon America was bogged down in an unconventional and dirty war that ruined its reputation and plummeted Johnson's popularity. There is no need to further describe this difficult period whose memory is still vivid and whose wounds are still open after almost half a century.

However, the spread of communism in the western hemisphere was a painful reality fomented by the Castro regime. In 1962, Juan Bosch of the leftist Dominican Revolutionary Party was elected president of the Dominican Republic, only to be overthrown by a military coup in 1963. The CIA was implicated in this operation.

Two years later, Bosch supporters launched a countercoup. Immediately Johnson ordered the U.S. Marines to land on that island and crush the pro-Bosch forces under the pretext that they were communists.

In 1966, Dr. Joaquin Balaguer was chosen as president in a rigged election, which began an on-and-off reign of thirty years marked by widespread repression and corruption.

Under Johnson's vigilant eyes, no spread of communism would be ever allowed in the American Continent.

The U.S. success on this backyard front was in sharp contrast to the failure in Vietnam. Even Johnson's great achievements on the domestic front (Civil Rights Act, Social Security Act, Voting Rights Act, just to mention a few) paled into insignificance when compared with that infamous and disastrous war.

Instead of carrying out a dream mission Johnson, the man with an incredible conviction (communism is intrinsically evil) and a great resolve to defeat it suffered an operational military nightmare. In spite of his undeniable political stature, the mounting protests at home and huge losses on Vietnamese soil made him a very unpopular president.

9
THE NIXON DOCTRINE

(January 20, 1969–August 9, 1974)

Richard Milhous Nixon (January 9, 1913–April 22, 1994) was the thirty-seventh President of the United States. He inherited from Johnson a nation in turmoil, including massive student protests and draft dodgers as well as a foreign policy in disarray, mostly over the Vietnam War.

Nixon did not shy away from his responsibilities as president and commander in chief. With his long experience in politics (in which he'd been elected to the House of Representatives in 1946 and the Senate in 1950, then vice president in 1952 under Dwight D. Eisenhower), he tackled both problems head on.

The unrest at home was caused by the lack of transparency in government policies and the military failure in Vietnam by the Americanization (deployment of American troops) of the war. In a November 3, 1969 address to the nation,[8] Nixon tried to rectify these two grave errors. With regard to transparency, he said:

---

[8] See Part Two, document 5, President Nixon's Speech on "Vietnamization", November 3, 1969.

I believe that one of the reasons for the deep divisions about Vietnam is that many Americans have lost confidence in what their Government has told them about our policy.

The American people cannot and should not be asked to support a policy which involves the overriding issues of war and peace unless they know the truth about that policy.

Therefore, Nixon, in a supreme effort to pacify and unite the Nation, was pledging candor and truth from his administration. He was promising there would be no dirty tricks, covert operations, or "two-faced" policies. He would be honest and sincere, explaining the reasons and objectives of his political moves and respecting the diversity of opinions of his opponents.

Nixon believed the Americanization of the war in Vietnam by the previous administration was wrong. He was therefore determined to change course via a slow withdrawal of American troops and an acceleration of the preparedness of Vietnamese forces, a process he called the *Vietnamization* of the war. South Vietnam would be totally in charge of its own defense although still counting on the support and expertise of the Americans.

Nixon summarized his doctrine:

First, the United States will keep all of its treaty commitments.

Second, we shall provide a shield if a nuclear power threatens the freedom of a nation allied with us or of a nation whose survival we consider vital to our security.

Third, in cases involving other types of aggression, we shall furnish military and economic assistance when requested in accordance with our treaty commitments. But we shall look to the nation directly threatened to assume the primary responsibility of providing the manpower for its defense.

The first point is a simple reaffirmation of American obligations and commitments.

The second point is a purposely vague representation regarding America's military engagement abroad. It is intentionally vague, undetermined, and undefined For example, what does "provide a shield" mean in practical terms? In determining what is "vital to our security," should the judgment be objective or subjective? In other words, should we be the only judges in this matter, or should we listen to the international community? In addition, "national security" is a very elastic term that can be stretched to the point of including a banana republic. Yet how could a banana republic be a threat to the security of America? It is clear that despite his previous representations of candor and truth, Nixon was a shrewd politician who did not want to be tied down by precise rules of engagement or clear norms of conduct.

In the third point of the summary, Nixon reaffirmed his conviction that each nation should assume the *primary responsibility* for its own defense, as America would no longer do so in its place.

Because of its generalities, the Nixon doctrine does not provide any new wrinkle in U.S. foreign policy. It is in perfect harmony with the previous doctrines, except for the "primary responsibility" language, which could be considered original and new as to Nixon if we disregard Kennedy's position. However, Kennedy actually followed the same principle without using any fancy word such as Vietnamization to designate the same reality.

To what extent was Nixon faithful to his own *doctrine of disengagement* and *pledge of transparency?* It is not easy to describe the events that took place between 1969 and 1973 as that was a very turbulent period.

While a partial withdrawal of troops was happening, secretly a heavy bombing had been initiated along Vietnam's borders with Cambodia. The aim of Operation Menu was to destroy the communist guerrilla sanctuaries. However, this campaign violated the repeated promises from Washington in support of Cambodia's neutrality. This operation was so massive and unprecedented that in the fourteen-month period, more tons of bombs were dropped than the total by the Allies in World War II.

While Nixon was trying to pacify the nation by promising "peace with honor" and calling on the "silent majority" to rally behind him, the invasion of Cambodia sparked protests nationwide in the United States. When members of the National Guard at Kent State University in Ohio killed four students, the outrage was immediate, adding more fuel to the antiwar movement.

Adding insult to injury, in 1971 the *New York Times* published a report on the top-secret U.S. involvement in Vietnam, detailing a long series of public deceptions. In the same year, an operation called Lam Son 719 by the pro-American Army of the Republic of Vietnam attempted to destroy the Ho Chi Minh trail in Laos. The offensive was a clear violation of Laos's neutrality and a disaster of monumental proportions. It represented the failure of Vietnamization as it showed that without American support, South Vietnam could not survive. Once again, a nation's neutrality had been violated, creating a dangerous instability with devastating consequences for both Cambodia and Laos.

If the mood at home with its antiwar protests was rebellious and frightening, the attitude within the ranks was not any better. Disobedience and fragging (murder of unpopular officers with fragmentation grenades) of officers increased considerably. To make matters worse, revelations were being made regarding the My Lai Massacre in which U.S. soldiers slaughtered countless civilians, including women and children. This sparked national and international outrage, destroying in the process the reputation and good name of America. Yet in spite of all this, in 1972 Nixon won reelection in one of the biggest landslide victories in U.S. political history.

Finally, on January 15, 1973, Nixon announced the suspension of hostilities towards North Vietnam. The Paris Peace Accords were signed on January 27, officially ending the American involvement in the Vietnam War. However, the only article of the Accord that was fully carried out was the total withdrawal of American forces from Vietnam.

Although sketchy, this synopsis provides an answer to the initial question: was Nixon faithful to his promises? The disengagement was implemented, not very convincingly but effectively. However, this is the only promise Nixon kept. His most important pledge of transparency and honesty was brutally eradicated by his callous disregard for the law of the land. Vietnamization failed miserably, and in fact, after the Americans left, South Vietnam fell into the hands of the communist North. The honor and respectability of America, one of the greatest priorities on Nixon's conscience, was irremediably compromised by his actions and those of U.S. soldiers during those years of cruel and senseless combat actions.

However, in spite of this somber panorama, Nixon's keen political intuition cannot be overlooked in his capturing the historical international moment in which he was living and making the best out of it. Riding on the "Red Scare" wave, Nixon rose to political prominence. When on the crest, he used his power and prestige to foster a détente with Russia and initiate a rapprochement with China.

For people who didn't live during that period, it might seem to have been a somewhat unusual time, but nothing extraordinary. However, for conservative religious politicians, that time was one of total madness and subversion of the scale of values. Nixon went from being an enraged and rabid anticommunist who wanted to bomb and obliterate any cell of Reds in Southeast Asia to becoming an engaged negotiator with Russia in the Strategic Arms Limitation Talks that resulted in the Salt I treaty and a promoter of a "Ping Pong Diplomacy" with China. This was quite a revolutionary change. For anyone with less personal involvement in people and events, it appears a brilliant move that defines Nixon's real political stature. When he observed the split between Russia and China, Nixon smelled the perfect opportunity to foster American interests with both countries while simultaneously reducing their support and aid to Vietnam.

Overall, Nixon was a true "Realpolitik man" who does not follow ideologies. Like a Renaissance man, in the genuine spirit of Machiavelli, he based his decisions on the actual historical situation and needs of his country rather than moral principles. In order to lessen international tensions and nuclear threats, he extended the hand of friendship to his archenemies, mindful that "today's foes are tomorrow's allies."

It is not easy to characterize Nixon. However, one of his contemporary and bitter political adversaries, Democratic Congresswoman Helen Gahagan Douglas, bestowed upon him one of the most colorful nicknames in American politics: "Tricky Dick." Without subscribing to this characterization, it is fair to say that Douglas, in a popular way, captured the complexity of Nixon's personality. Political blunders (secret bombings and Watergate) aside, Nixon should be remembered as an intelligent and shrewd political figure who reinvented himself several times in order to survive in the difficult arena of public affairs.

He was not a charismatic or visionary leader who inspires legions of people, but a cool and calculating man, ready to sacrifice his own mother in order to achieve his goals.

He was not a hardcore conservative, preaching and sticking to his principles against all odds, but someone flexible and realistic.

He did not set forth any surprising new doctrine, just a revolutionary praxis with a powerful message to all present and future leaders of the world: "Read the signs of the time. Do not cloud your judgment with ideologies, religious views, or preconceived ideas. Do not be afraid. Be brave and innovative."

This is how Nixon should be remembered and celebrated.

10
THE CARTER DOCTRINE

(January 20, 1977–January 20, 1981)

The Carter doctrine is basically an extension of the Truman doctrine and can be summarized with his own words:

> Let our position be absolutely clear: An attempt by any outside force to gain control of the Persian Gulf region will be regarded as an assault on the vital interests of the United States of America, and such an assault will be repelled by any means necessary, including military force.

Author Daniel Yergin[9] observes that the Carter doctrine is quite similar to a 1903 British declaration. The then-foreign secretary Lord Lansdowne warned Russia and Germany that the British would "regard the establishment of a naval base or of a fortified port in the Persian Gulf by any other power as a very grave menace to British interests, and we should certainly resist it with all the means at our disposal."

---

[9] Yergin, Daniel. *The Prize: The Epic Quest for Oil, Money and Power*. New York: Simon & Schuster, 1991.

It would appear that the Carter doctrine lacked significance and originality; moreover, it appeared lost in Carter's State of the Union Address (the last of his presidency) as other concerns took center stage. However, appearances are deceiving. Without a doubt, the January 23, 1980 speech[10] not only shed abundant light on Carter's political doctrine, but also on his overall personality. This speech is his last legacy as president, constituting an impassioned plea for humanity, a poignant cry for sanity in international relations, and a supreme message of goodwill and extension of a helping hand for humankind.

Despite having all the power of the president of the United States of America, Carter is neither cocky nor arrogant like some before him and others after. He is a conciliatory voice for *peace, freedom* and *human rights*. As a ruler, he was a monument to wisdom; as a man, he is a powerful inspirator to *ad astra per aspera* (through difficulties to the stars) and a magnet to everything that is human and noble.

Unlike presidents before him whose overall concern seemed to be maintaining some kind of superior posture seeking domination of the free and democratic world, Jimmy Carter described a new leadership role for his country:

> I'm determined that the United States will remain the strongest of all nations, but our power will never be used to *initiate a threat to the security of any nation or to the rights of any human being*. We seek to be and to remain secure—a nation at peace in a stable world.

Carter is definitely for peace, freedom, and human rights. Without freedom, there is no peace, and without human rights, any freedom is purely illusory.

Jimmy Carter worked tirelessly for peace.

During his first month in office, he cut the defense budget by $6 billion. One of his first acts was to unilaterally remove all nuclear weapons from South Korea and cut back the number of U.S. troops stationed there. When Major General John K. Singlaub publicly criticized these decisions, he was promptly relieved of duty.

---

[10] See Part Two, document 6, Jimmy Carter: State of the Union Address 1980.

Undoubtedly, Carter's biggest accomplishments in the area of peace were the Camp David Accords reached on September 17, 1978. These constituted a peace agreement between Israel and Egypt that was followed by the signing of a peace treaty on March 26, 1979. Incredibly, a neighboring Arab nation was now at peace with Israel.

Carter's ultimate goal in this troubled area was the creation of a Palestinian state accepted by Israel and the international community. Unfortunately, even after many more years this noble objective remains elusive.

To show his firm commitment to peace, Carter negotiated with Russia to substantially reduce the nuclear arms produced and maintained by both countries. Towards the end of 1979, Carter and Leonid Brezhnev reached an agreement, the SALT II treaty. However, after the Russian invasion of Afghanistan, Carter withdrew the treaty from consideration by Congress. Yet although the treaty was never ratified, both sides honored their commitments.

As he stated in his inaugural address, Carter's greatest aspiration was to banish completely any nuclear weapon from the face of the earth. This would have meant a step closer to world peace.

Removing today's roots of discontent means to sow the seeds of tomorrow's peace. In one of his most controversial moves, in September 1977 Carter signed the Panama Canal Treaty that essentially transferred control of the American-built Panama Canal to the nation of Panama.

Without detracting anything from these great achievements, President Jimmy Carter showed himself to be a man totally dedicated to peace during the two most disturbing crises of his presidency: the *Iran hostage crisis*, and the *invasion of Afghanistan by the Soviet Union.*

The Iran hostage crisis had its roots in the Iranian Revolution's overthrowing of the Shah of Iran, Mohammad Reza Pahlavi, America's strongest ally since World War II. However, America did not intervene in favor of its ally, and Carter initially refused to grant the Shah asylum. Finally, on October 22, 1979, the president on humanitarian grounds gave the Shah temporary permission to be in the United States for the duration of his cancer treatment. In response, Iranian militants seized the American embassy in Teheran. Fifty-two Americans were taken hostage as the militants presented a list of demands.

Carter's overall strategy was to freeze all Iranian assets and try to rescue the hostages without casualties or bloodshed. The failed rescue attempt by military means contributed to Carter's being defeated in his reelection bid in 1980. The president's popularity reached its lowest point as the popular perception of him was that he was weak and a loser. (This is despite the fact that through difficult and prolonged negotiations, Carter secured the release of all hostages.) The man of peace prevailed by sacrificing his own reputation and good name. He saved the others (the Shah and the hostages) by giving up his own political life. There is no greater love than this.

Almost simultaneously with the Iranian crisis, the Soviet Union in December 1979 invaded Afghanistan. This double punch could have had devastating consequences not just for the United States but the entire free world. To allow the Russian army to establish a firm foothold in Afghanistan could have meant the destabilization of the Persian Gulf region, which in turn would have jeopardized the oil supply. Therefore Carter declared the Gulf region off limits to any outside power and promised military intervention if this edict were violated.

Given these ominous precedents coupled with a deteriorating economy at home (loss of jobs, economic stagnation, and high interest with price inflation), Carter could have been expected to take some radical initiatives. After all, both his popularity and his political future were at stake as his reelection year loomed.

However, Carter neither listened to his many critics clamoring for military intervention in Afghanistan nor followed the blind forces of his injured ego. As with the Iranian crisis, he proceeded cautiously. He imposed drastic sanctions on the Russians, including both economic (he cut the export of wheat, very unpopular with American farmers) and cultural. He caused the United States to boycott the Olympic Games in Moscow and froze diplomatic relations.

On top of this, Carter reinstated registration for the draft. As a man of principles and Christian convictions, he did not follow the easy way. Instead, he took without flinching, the most unpopular measures. His primary goal was peace, not being reelected. Faithful to his program and values, he paid the ultimate price. Yet in spite of it all, his heart remained in the right place.

Jimmy Carter worked tirelessly for freedom and human rights. He made *freedom from tyranny* and *respect for human rights* his trademarks. What is more, he declared human rights as being part of our national interest: "That is why *our support for human rights in other countries is in our own national interest as well as part of our own national character.*" Nobody before (and probably nobody after) Carter will ever dare to formulate such a principle that expressed one of his deepest convictions.

Not only did Carter make the support of human rights in other countries into our own national interest, but also he identified it as being part of our national character. As a nation, we were born with this, as something embedded in our DNA. If we renounce our support of human rights, we renounce our own identity, and we would no longer be true Americans.

From this stems the originality of Carter doctrine that nobody has ever stressed or pointed out. It would be redundant to say that he put his money where is mouth was, because his entire life during and after the presidency was dedicated to the support of *human rights* all over the world. No American president was ever as active in the international scene after leaving office as Carter has been.

He is the modern apostle of all that is human, honest, moral, and principled.

The world has always been plagued by tyrants, dictators, and abusers of basic human rights. It is impossible to make right all the wrongs. However, in this field, Carter has been a real innovator, reversing a long-held U.S. policy of supporting strong men who were American allies. On Carter's agenda, containment was no longer the number one priority as human rights now occupied that place. Accordingly, Carter ended support to the Nicaraguan dictator Anastasio Somoza. He continued his predecessors' policies of imposing sanctions on Rhodesia. Strong pressure from the United States and United Kingdom prompted new elections in Zimbabwe Rhodesia (now Zimbabwe). After Robert Mugabe was elected Prime Minister, the sanctions were lifted and full diplomatic relations established. Carter also strongly criticized the apartheid government of South Africa, Alfredo Stroessner's dictatorship in Paraguay, the military repression in Chile by Augusto Pinochet (whose ascent to power had been previously orchestrated by the Americans), and the corruption of Omar Torrijos in Panama.

Unfortunately, Carter did not listen to Archbishop Oscar Romero's pleas not to send military aid to El Salvador. Yet in spite of this and other oversights, Carter remains a great champion of human rights, an intrepid defender of the oppressed, and a believable voice for the silenced all over the world.

After leaving office, Carter has dedicated his life to pursue the noble ideals of peace, freedom, and human rights. To this shining crown he added a new precious gem, Habitat for Humanity. Since 1984, he has been involved in this organization via fund-raising and, what is deeply moving, by actually building homes like any other humble construction worker. It is quite a sight to see a former U.S. president with a helmet on his head and a tool belt around his waist hammering nails, cementing bricks, and lifting wooden structures under the burning sun.

In recognition of his outstanding contribution to world peace, in 2002 he was awarded the Nobel Peace Prize.

Jimmy Carter's lasting legacy transcends time and space. It goes beyond any political doctrine or fancy theory. It is a spirit that should inspire any person in power and serve as a supreme model for any human being. He showed how power can serve peace, freedom, and human rights. He represents the best of America as the greatest unsung politician of modern times.

11

THE REAGAN DOCTRINE

(January 20, 1981–January 20, 1989)

In a first superficial reading of his personality, Ronald Reagan presented himself, as a lovable human being full of humor and understanding, one with a simplified vision of a world clearly divided into good and evil, black and white—we free people and you undemocratic nations. He seemed ready to take on the world with a trigger-happy attitude such as the one we see in his movies.

However, if we scratch the surface, we realize that nothing could be further from the truth. As much as Reagan appeared transparent and straightforward, his inward persona was complicated and convoluted.

Two major factors contributed to this Reagan's complex personality: his *career as an actor*, and his *switching to the Republican Party* from the Democratic in 1962 at the age of fifty-one.

As an actor, he portrayed different characters who obviously did not always reflect his inner feelings or ideals. He learned to hide himself masterfully behind these make-believe heroes of the big screen. As a politician, he never abandoned completely his Democratic soul. According to his own confession: "I didn't leave the Democratic Party—the party left me." He never became a radical Republican, as he never lost completely his Democratic leanings.

In this fascinating personality, we can uncover clear traces of deep humanity and sincere compassion stemming from his original soul, as well as traces of sophistication that at times become manipulation and outright trickery, the product of his newly acquired soul.

His political doctrine can be better understood in the light of his Secretary of State doctrine and in his mystifying psychological chiaroscuro. Through these two filters, Reagan's mind and actions acquire transparency and logic that otherwise would be absent. In his case, his dual soul didn't create a double personality; on the contrary, it gave life to a charming and likeable person.

The great goals of the Reagan Administration were formulated repeatedly and with extreme clarity. Domestically, the economic situation with high unemployment and a staggering inflation rate had to be tackled head-on following a few basic principles, inspired by a supply-side economics and a laissez-faire philosophy: *less government intervention and fewer taxes.* By reducing the growth of domestic government spending, cutting back on excessive regulations, and instituting a sound currency policy to end inflation, Reagan was making a clear departure from his immediate predecessors.

This economic policy, dubbed "Reaganomics," was the subject of many debates. Supporters pointed to improvements in certain key economic indicators while critics stressed the staggering federal budget deficits and increasing national debt. This "trickle-down economics" as it was labeled by his critics was based on the belief that if the taxes on the wealthy were reduced, the beneficial effects would "trickle down" to the poor and improve their economic situation. On the one hand, it was clear that the wealthy benefited enormously from this policy. On the other hand, is not so clear that the poor got any benefit from it, and some critics swore the poor became worse off.

Reagan's economic policies might be susceptible of a double and contrasting interpretation, but not so his actions. One stands out that shows unmistakably whose side the president was on.

Only a short time after Reagan was sworn in, the federal air traffic controllers went on strike, violating a regulation that prohibited government unions from striking. With firmness and decisiveness, Reagan gave them an ultimatum: either report to work within forty-eight hours or be fired. In spite of mounting fears in his Cabinet of a political backlash and the enormous risks of disrupting a vital sector of transportation, on August 5, 1981, the president fired 11,345 air traffic controllers, breaking the union. The message was clear for everybody, but particularly employers in the private sectors: it was all right to go up against the unions.

In another matter, a piece of legislation, the Immigration Reform and Control Act (IRCA) that seemed to favor the workers (mainly immigrants), was just a subtle move geared towards improving the economic situation. By prohibiting employers from hiring illegal immigrants and by granting amnesty to almost three million of them, Reagan eliminated a large underground economy that was not benefiting the federal government. His justification—"the legalization provisions in this act will go far to improve the lives of a class of individuals who now must hide in the shadows"—is a masterful camouflaging of his real intentions. To this day, Reagan and the Republican Party are perceived as favoring the rich while abandoning the poor to destitution.

If domestically the Reagan doctrine was clear, no less transparent was his international stand. Internationally, Reagan as the supreme leader of the free world was preaching his special brand of doctrine, which was based on spreading freedom and democracy by rolling back the communist expansion. This is the cornerstone of his political doctrine: *spread democracy and freedom*, and *shrink or roll back the communist expansion.* Reagan was the great apostle of a new political religion, ready to set the world on fire. His preaching, flowing from the lips of the Great Communicator as he was known, left no one unmoved. It was colorful and inspiring.

In his first inaugural address,[11] Reagan presented in a handful of superb brushstrokes the overall philosophy that inspired his foreign policy. As an "exemplar of freedom" and "beacon of hope," Americans would strengthen their ties with neighbors and allies without ever imposing on their sovereignty. As for enemies and potential adversaries, they should know that peace was the highest aspiration of the American people. However, although Americans can negotiate or sacrifice for it, they would never surrender for it—now or ever. American reluctance to engage in conflict and war should never be

---

[11] See Part Two, document 7a, Ronald Reagan: Excerpt from the Inaugural Address January 20, 1981.

misunderstood or misjudged as a lack of will, because the best weapon in the formidable arsenal of the United States is precisely the indomitable will and moral courage of free men and women. He also wanted it known that Americans possessed the most sophisticated material weapons and the finest moral arms in the world.

Reagan's supreme ideals and values are freedom rooted on peace and strength anchored on free will and moral courage. War should be the last resort—one engaged in only when everything else has failed.

Not less compelling and overwhelming is the message in Regan's second inaugural address.[12] A few paragraphs convey a taste of Reagan's mastery in conveying the best of humanity in words that spring from his heart:

> We believe faith and freedom must be our guiding stars, for they show us truth, they make us brave, give us hope, and leave us wiser than we were.
>
> Harry Truman once said that, ultimately, our security and the world's hopes for peace and human progress lie not in measures of defense or in the control of weapons, but in the growth and expansion of freedom and self-government.
>
> And tonight, we declare anew to our fellow citizens of the world: *Freedom is not the sole prerogative of a chosen few; it is the universal right of all God's children.* Look to where peace and prosperity flourish today. It is in homes that freedom built. Victories against poverty are greatest and peace, most secure where people live by laws that ensure free press, free speech, and freedom to worship, vote, and create wealth.
>
> Our mission is to nourish and defend freedom and democracy, and to communicate these ideals everywhere we can.

Reagan was a new paladin of democracy and a new champion of freedom. Not all this fervor of a modern crusader to defend the

---

[12] See Part Two, document 7b, Ronald Reagan, Address to the Nation, February 6, 1985.

universal right to freedom remains in the abstract world of ideals. Our president was aware that "we cannot play innocents abroad in a world that's not innocent; nor can we be passive when freedom is under siege. Without resources, diplomacy cannot succeed."

For this reason, Reagan mounted a formidable machine of *moral*, *economic*, and *military* support to any group or nation, from Afghanistan to Nicaragua, "to defy Soviet-supported aggression and secure rights which have been ours from birth." It is here where his marvelous world of values and principles must be coupled with concrete implementation and verified to see if the second measures up to the great expectations of the first. After all, what defines the true nature of a man are not his words, however inspiring they might be, but his actions. In this minefield of overt and covert operations, of military actions and economic support, we shall discover the real stature of Ronald Reagan.

His sphere of influence spanned from Latin America to Asia and Africa, and in particular in Afghanistan, Angola, Cambodia, Ethiopia, Iran, Laos, Lebanon, Libya, Nicaragua, Vietnam and Grenada. Four major interventions captured Reagan's complex personality, revealing in depth his dual soul.

The first is Lebanon. On October 23, 1983, the American peacekeeping forces (a contingent of a multinational force in Beirut) were the victims of suicide bombers who killed 241 American servicemen. This was the deadliest single-day death toll in the Marines since the battle of Iwo Jima and the deadliest single-day massacre of the U.S. military since the first day of the Tet offensive in January 1968. This despicable act would have provoked any warmonger to retaliate on a grand scale. The obliteration of the Sheik Abdullah barracks in Baalbek, Lebanon, which housed Iranian Revolutionary Guards believed to be training Hezbollah fighters, would have seemed an appropriate response.

But Reagan was well aware of the volatility of that corner of the world, which was becoming a powder keg. Mindful of the Weinberger Doctrine set forth by Secretary of Defense Casper Weinberger, the president aborted a retaliatory mission. As was more in tune with his Democratic soul, on February 7, 1984, he ordered the Marines to start withdrawing from Lebanon.

The second event involved the invasion of Grenada. On October l3, a Marxist-Leninist faction aligned with the Soviet Union and Cuba seized power. On October 25, 1983, two days after the Beirut massacre, Reagan ordered the invasion of Grenada. The official reasons for the invasion were the formal appeal from the Organization of Eastern Caribbean States (OECS), the threat posed by a Soviet-Cuban buildup in the Caribbean, and the concern for the safety of several hundreds of American students on the island.

However, behind that sudden move was something more than the fear of communism or concern for American lives. Reagan wanted to send a strong message to his adversaries that he could be tough whenever he chose to be. Although he would not be dragged into a conflict that did not conform to his parameters, he was in charge, and he would not be pushed around.

The invasion of Grenada was the first major U.S. military operation since the Vietnam War, and it was a total success. The loss of American lives was minimal (nineteen fatalities and 116 wounded), and communism was swept away for good from that Caribbean island.

The third event involved retaliation against Libya. The year 1986 began ominously for Reagan. The disintegration of the space shuttle *Challenger* on January 28, 1986, left all the nation shocked and in tears. On the same night of the disaster, instead of giving his State of the Union Address, Reagan delivered a soothing speech to alleviate the immense national pain. He rose to the occasion in a marvelous way. That was Reagan at his best.

In early April 1986, a bomb exploded in a Berlin discotheque. Sixty-three American military personnel were injured, and one serviceman was killed. Reagan was convinced Libya was behind this terrorist bombing. On April 15, 1986, he launched a series of air strikes on Libyan soil designed to render inoperable Muammar Gaddafi's ability to export terrorism. The justification was clear: "When our citizens are attacked or abused anywhere in the world on the direct orders of hostile regimes, we will respond so long as I'm in this office." Once again, in the face of provocation, Reagan showed determination, but at the same time, restraint and shrewdness.

The fourth crisis in Reagan's presidency was the Iran-Contra Affair. The fatal year of 1986 was marred by the largest U.S. political scandal of the l980s. The story possesses a Byzantine complexity of incredible proportions due to the different parties involved and the twisted way the operation was conducted. In an oversimplified summary, the main objective of the Reagan Administration was to roll back communism and offer economic and military aid to anticommunist movements all over the world. His administration engaged in a covert operation of selling arms to Iran to fund Contra insurgents in Nicaragua even though this had been specifically made illegal by an act of Congress.

Thus, aid to the Contras was an illegal activity carried out by the American Government. The final result was good, but the modality lay outside the law. Would the end justify the means?

As soon as it surfaced, the scandal rocked the Reagan Administration. The president emphatically denied having any knowledge of the affair, but his popularity went from 67 percent to 46 percent in less than a week, the quickest decline ever for a president.

Reagan appointed a commission to investigate the scandal. The results were surprising, not for the fourteen indictments and eleven convictions (including Secretary of State, Caspar Weinberger), but for the lack of evidence tying Reagan with the scandal. It was hardly credible that the great architect of the support of anticommunist movements around the world and the closer of the Cold War era with the falling of the Berlin wall ("Mr. Gorbachev, tear down this wall") was completely extraneous to that arms sale. However, Washington insiders did not find this surprising as it is a well-established practice to carry out controversial operations without implicating the commander in chief.

Reagan had dedicated body and soul to that extraordinary cause, and he was ready to do anything—as he unfortunately did—to achieve the coveted goal. The commission findings may have diffused a potential impeachment case against him, but they cast a large shadow on Reagan's honesty and integrity. Reagan was well intentioned when he was preaching freedom and democracy, but regrettably, he was not well intentioned when he tried to implement his words.

Thus, Reagan's dual soul is one of the main keys to interpreting his complex personality. On the one hand, Regan had a sublime and idealistic vision of sacrificing anything in order to defeat tyranny and dictatorships and achieve freedom and democracy. However, on the other hand, he was willing to engage in illegal and deceitful acts in sharp contrast to those noble ideals.

12

THE WEINBERGER DOCTRINE

(January 21, 1981–November 23, 1987)

A better understanding of Reagan's personality can be gained from a look at the doctrine set forth by his secretary of defense as the Weinberger Doctrine constitutes a major interpretational key to Reagan's political decisions and his overall foreign policy. Without this outstanding cabinet member, the Reagan Administration would have certainly charted a different course in the Beirut massacre, Libya bombing, Grenada invasion, and Iran-Contra Affair.

Born in San Francisco, California, Weinberger obtained his BA magna cum laude in 1938 and his JD in 1941, both from Harvard University. He enlisted in the U.S. Army as a private in the same year of his graduation and served in the 41st Infantry Division in the Pacific until the end of the war.

Weinberger showed a great interest in politics and history, working in California as an assemblyman under Governor Ronald Reagan. In 1970, he moved to Washington and served under Richard Nixon as director of the Office of Management and Budget and Secretary of Health, Education and Welfare.

In 1981, Reagan nominated him as Secretary of Defense. On November 23, 1987, Caspar resigned, alleging his wife's declining health. The real reason was the disclosure of the Iran-Contra Affair and increased difficulties with the Department of Defense budget. He was indicted, charged with several felony counts of lying to the Iran-Contra independent counsel.

On December 24, 1992, he received a presidential pardon from outgoing President George H. W. Busch.

If his historical trajectory as man and politician may seem more than ordinary and indeed almost remarkable, his contribution to the American political doctrine should have a special place in history and an everlasting influence on any man with the awesome responsibility of guiding a nation. Nobody before Caspar Weinberger had ever shown a better insight into contemporary history or formulated clearer principles for a military action. His doctrine and his practical guidelines should constitute a political reference guide not just for anyone aspiring to be a politician, but for anyone interested in the American spirit.

In his famous 1984 speech, "The Uses of Military Power,"[13] Weinberger lays out with clarity and conciseness his main beliefs. The analysis of the political situation of his times captures the essence of what will be known years later as the post 9/11 terrorist atmosphere.

During World War II and before, the lines between war and peace, friends and foes, values and abominations were clear. The whole nation, including its industries and families, was behind its soldiers, working and sacrificing for them. However, now the lines between open conflict and half-hidden acts are so blurred that "we cannot confidently predict where, or when, or how, or from what direction aggression may arrive." The new enemy does not represent any particular nation and does not have an identifiable face.

While America's top priority is to work for peace avoiding conflicts, it must be prepared, at any moment, to meet "threats ranging in intensity from isolated terrorist acts, to guerrilla action, to full-scale military confrontation." When and how the use of military force is acceptable remains an unresolved question. In spite of this theoretical gray area, America must avoid two extreme positions: isolationism and the urge to resolve all the conflicts of the world. At the end, both

---

[13] See Part Two, document 8, Casper W. Weinberger "The Uses of Military Power," November 28, 1984.

positions are going to be more costly than any reasonable and supported military intervention.

The two main elements that justify a war are *national security and vital national interests in imminent danger*, and *strong consensus of support and agreement by Congress and the U.S. people*. This consensus of support is so fundamental that without it we tear at the fabric of our society, creating turmoil and riots in our cities (as occurred during the Vietnam War), and we provoke the scorn of our troops reducing their morale and their effectiveness. The importance of this consensus of support can never be adequately stressed or emphasized.

However, if this national consensus is of paramount importance, no less fundamental is *international support*. America is not the world's defender and should not substitute people in their fighting for survival. According to Weinberger:

> Recent history has proven that we cannot assume unilaterally the role of the world's defender ....So while we may and should offer substantial amounts of economic and military assistance to our allies in their time of need, and help them maintain forces to deter attacks against them usually we cannot substitute our troops or our will for theirs.

Before sending U.S. combat forces abroad, Weinberger believed America should keep in mind these six basic requirements:

> First, the United States should not commit forces to combat overseas unless the particular engagement or occasion is deemed vital to our national interest or that of our allies.

> Second, if we decide it is necessary to put combat troops into a given situation, we should do so wholeheartedly, and with the clear intention of winning. If we are unwilling to commit the forces or resources necessary to achieve our objectives, we should not commit them at all.

> Third, if we do decide to commit forces to combat overseas, we should have clearly defined political and military objectives.

And we should know precisely how our forces can accomplish those clearly defined objectives.

Fourth, the relationship between our objectives and the forces we have committed, their size, composition and disposition must be continually reassessed and adjusted if necessary. Conditions and objectives invariably change during the course of a conflict. When they do change, then so must our combat requirements.

Fifth, before the U.S. commits combat forces abroad, there must be some reasonable assurance we will have the support of the American people and their elected representatives in Congress.

Finally, the commitment of U.S. forces to combat should be a last resort.

The requirements are clear: national interest, total commitment, well-defined political and military objectives, flexibility according to the changing circumstances, and support by the American people. Force should be used only as a last resort. "When we ask our military forces to risk their very lives in such situations, a note of caution is not only prudent, it is *morally required*."

Obviously, these well-thought out requirements, conditions, or prerequisites are not exclusive or entirely comprehensive, but neither are they absolute or unreachable. They are certainly powerful guidelines that can facilitate the awesome task of the president's deciding whether a military action is required.

How many war engagements could have been avoided if these prerequisites had been enforced? In addition, and more importantly, how many human lives could have been spared, and how much misery and suffering could have been avoided?

Caspar Weinberger should be remembered as a great war theoretician, whose best interest at heart was America's safety and prosperity while he carried out a popular mandate with international approval. However, although his principles were reasonable, clear, and compelling, his implementation was not totally in line with his theory.

As it so often happens, real life does not always follow sublime preaching. Then, stumbling is inevitable and ruinous, as occurred in the Iran-Contra Affair.

13

THE CLINTON DOCTRINE

(January 20, 1993–January 20, 2001)

Undoubtedly, in the gallery of American presidents, Bill Clinton occupies a special place. He is the ultimate comeback kid of politics—impressive in the glorious days of success, and unforgettable during the darkest hours of his impeachment.

President Clinton stands out for his Third Way philosophy, described as centrist. He presided over the longest period of peacetime economic expansion. He left office after balancing the budget and creating a considerable surplus.

In spite of being impeached by the U.S. House of Representatives for perjury and obstruction of justice in the Monica Lewinsky scandal, he was acquitted by the Senate and left office with an approval rating at 65 percent, the highest end-of- office rating of anyone since the end of World War II.

His presidency was remarkable in many ways as was his personality full of charm and charisma. The first baby boomer president did not have a war experience. His approach to politics was mainly a carrot-style rather than a big stick approach. His way of conducting foreign policy stopped the decline of the image of America abroad.

The military actions carried out during his second term in office reflected his overall strategy of moderation, deterrence, and serious warning. A bombing campaign against Saddam Hussein, Operation Desert Fox, lasted from December 16 to December 19, 1998. Its clear aim was to destabilize Hussein's government and make him lose his grip on power, thus preparing the Iraqi nation for a change of regime.

A second bombing operation called Operation Allied Force took place under the NATO umbrella in 1999. Its purpose was to stop the ethnic cleansing and genocide of Albanians in Kosovo by nationalist Serbians during the presidency of Slobodan Milošević.

The operation was highly successful with the military losses negligible. Today Kosovo is independent from Serbia.

This absence of a real war where American troops were committed abroad and suffered terrible casualties explains not only the lack of originality in the Clinton doctrine, but also its almost nonexistence. As odd as it might seem, Clinton neither possessed a personal doctrine nor did he ever put forward anything original in this field. Apparently because of the political reality he was living in, his priorities lay somewhere else. What is designated as Clinton doctrine should be more appropriately called "development of the previous interventionism."

In his lengthy February 26, 1999 speech in San Francisco[14] on foreign policy, he talked about the first challenge in building a more peaceful twenty-first century world and incidentally expressed his convictions regarding American interventionism:

> It's easy, for example, to say that we really have no interests in who lives in this or that valley in Bosnia, or who owns a strip of brushland in the Horn of Africa, or some piece of parched earth by the Jordan River. But the true measure of our interests lies not in how small or distant these places are, or in whether we have trouble pronouncing their names. The question we must ask is what are the consequences to our security of letting conflicts fester and spread. *We cannot, indeed, we should not, do everything or be everywhere.* However, where we can make a difference, we must be prepared to do so. And we must

---

[14] See Part Two, document 9, Remarks by President Bill Clinton on Foreign Policy.

remember that the real challenge of foreign policy is to deal with problems before they harm our national interests.

According to Clinton, even the smallest trouble in a faraway and unpronounceable strip of foreign land can affect American national interests. The government's task is seeing in advance the dangerous consequences of letting a problem spread. However, it should be clear that America does not have to intervene everywhere and solve all the problems of the planet.

The central peace of every American doctrine has always been national interests jointly with freedom and democracy. Clinton seemed at first to widen the national interests area to include any troubled corner of the world, but later on, he reduced its scope with the generic statement, "We should not be everywhere." Ultimately, it is up to presidential wisdom to decide what is the national interest and what is not, and when to intervene and when not.

Clinton's pronouncement did not bring anything new or original to the doctrine of interventionism. To the contrary, he left things purposely fuzzy and vague like before.

Clinton was not interested in putting forward a doctrine. This, in fact, was directly connected to his view on military intervention. A "draft dodger" like Clinton is very unsympathetic to war and any military interventions. He was convinced that a bellicose attitude was counterproductive and that war is not the appropriate tool to solve conflicts.

> It is in our interest to be a peacemaker, not because we think we can make all these differences go away, but because, in over 200 years of hard effort here at home, we have learned that the world works better when differences are resolved by the force of argument rather than the force of arms.

The Clintonian frame of mind, in which the force of argument is far superior to the force of arms, can hardly be stressed enough. It represents a clear departure from his predecessors and stands out like a superb milestone, signifying the best of a forgotten American soul. If every one of the previous presidents was ready to fight for peace, freedom, and democracy, none of them (except Jimmy Carter) was ready to convert the swords into ploughs. Clinton was determined to present a hopeful vision of the future where the deafening sound of the bombs and the deadly hissing of the bullets would no longer frighten people, including children and the elderly.

Clintons stands out and should be remembered as the man without a doctrine, but with a powerful vision of the twenty-first century. In this vision, the young and charismatic president presents the exciting challenges that America, as a whole should face and take up.

> Our *first challenge* is to build a more peaceful twenty-first century world. To that end, we're renewing alliances that extend the area where wars do not happen, and working to stop the conflicts that are claiming lives and threatening our interests right now.

In that sense, Clinton was pushing hard for NATO's enlargement, building a stronger alliance with Japan, and intensifying efforts for a genuine peace in Korea. The crown jewels of his efforts for peace were the Good Friday Accord and the Middle East Accord. We should never forget those two memorable days.

In the first (April 10, 1998), Ireland, Northern Ireland, and Great Britain witnessed the end of a bloody period, where bombings, terrorist acts, and massacres were a daily occurrence. In the second (September 13, 1993), something unthinkable happened: the leaders of Israel and the Palestinian Authority together signed a peace accord in the White House. This was the reason Clinton intended to use his time in office to push for a comprehensive peace settlement in the Middle East.

Another hot spot, the Balkans (Bosnia in particular) saw his efforts for a lasting peace:

> Kosovo is not an easy problem. However, if we do not stop the conflict now, it clearly will spread. And then we will not be able to stop it, except at far greater cost and risk."

> The *second challenge* we face is to bring our former adversaries, Russia and China, into the international system as open, prosperous, stable nations. The way both countries

develop in the coming century will have a lot to do with the future of our planet.

The Russians will decide their own future. However, the American people must work with them for the best possible outcome, with realism and with patience. China must also face the question of assuring stability and progress for its people. Will it choose openness and engagement, or will it limit the aspirations of its people without fully embracing global rules? Only the first path is a viable solution.

Our third great challenge is to build a future in which our people are safe from the dangers that arise, perhaps halfway around the world—dangers from proliferation, from terrorism, from drugs, from the multiple catastrophes that could arise from climate change.

The biggest threats of the new century weren't nuclear strikes from Russia or China, but the proliferation and use of weapons of mass destruction by an outlaw nation or a terrorist group. The Clinton Administration made every effort to keep Saddam Hussein's Iraq in check. Even though it would take years, every terrorist individual or group must now know there is no place to hide.

Another important task was to train police and medical personnel to deal effectively with chemical, biological, and nuclear emergencies. The computer system, so critical in the daily functioning of any organization, had to be made safer against sabotage and hackers. A national missile system is in the works against threats from rogue nations.

An international unified effort must be undertaken to protect people from the scourge of *drugs*. These constitute a real danger to democracy and national security.

Another global danger is *climate change*. In 1997, a new giant step forward was made when America helped to forge the Kyoto agreement, reducing emissions of greenhouse gases.

Our fourth challenge is to create a world trading and financial system that will lift the lives of ordinary people on every continent around the world.

Clinton's dream was to put a human face on the global economy. Globalization was irreversible, and if not humanized in a rational system it could create more inequalities and depravation.

> We are working to build a trading system that upholds the rights of workers and consumers, and helps us and them in other countries to protect the environment.

Finally, "Our fifth challenge has to keep freedom as a top goal for the world of the twenty-first century."

> Therefore, beyond economics, beyond the transformation of the great countries to economic security—Russia and China—beyond many of our security concerns, we also have to recognize that we can have no greater purpose than to support the right of other people to live in freedom and shape their own destiny. If that right could be universally exercised, virtually every goal I have outlined today would be advanced.

Interdependence, fraternization, and *helping hand* are the key terms for the new millennium, not superiority, domination, and war.

> For our nation to be strong, we must maintain a consensus that seemingly distant problems can come home if they are not addressed, and addressed promptly. We must recognize we cannot lift ourselves to heights to which we aspire if the world is not rising with us. I say again, the inexorable logic of globalization is the genuine recognition of interdependence. We cannot wish into being the world we seek. Talk is cheap; decisions are not.

There is no better conclusion to this unparallel vision than Clinton's own words: "In an interdependent world, we cannot lead if we expect to lead only on our own terms, and never on our own nickel. We can't be a first-class power if we're only prepared to pay for steerage."

The true world superpower shows its strength and superiority not by imposing its decisions by coercion and blackmail, but by forging agreements and coalitions beneficial to everybody. Only by saving the others will America save itself from decline and destruction. Clinton could not have formulated a better program for America, injecting a genuine humanitarian spirit. The human race is one and indivisible. Either we work and save together, or we fight each other and perish together.

14

THE BUSH DOCTRINE

(January 20, 2001–January 20, 2009)

George Walker Bush is the forty-third president of the United States of America. He entered into the political scene with an unconvincing victory, following such illustrious predecessors as Ronald Reagan and Secretary of Defense Caspar Weinberger, his father, George Herbert Walker Bush, and mainly Bill Clinton—all very knowledgeable, moderate, and extremely tactful in foreign policy. This would have suggested the Bush administration would be intent on building bridges and patching up differences diplomatically.

However quite to the contrary, instead of swinging towards moderation and reconciliation, the historical pendulum with Bush took a sharp turn in the opposite direction, inaugurating a dark period of confrontation with all the major powers and international organizations. This stemmed from Bush's critical decision to topple the brutal Iraqi dictator Saddam Hussein.

The whole world was shocked and stood silent, asking how this could happen. How could a man professing Christian beliefs, with a good and amicable nature, a spontaneous sense of humor and mild manners, reach the point of engaging in a war that would prove so costly and divisive? It appears incomprehensible, almost beyond human reason and common sense for outsiders and those not in tune with Washington politics or extraneous to the powerful Pentagon policy makers and advisers.

However, this mystery can be partially solved by examining an important document, "Defense Policy Guidance 1992–1994," which was a blueprint for the September 2000 "Rebuilding America's Defenses Strategy, Forces and Resources for a New Century."[15] In addition, the recrudescent forms of religious radicalism in America and particularly in the Arab world, as represented by the cataclysmic events of September 11, 2001, offer a reasonable explanation of the Bush Administration's abrupt departure from the traditional doctrine. Finally, the composition of Bush's Cabinet, with Dick Cheney (the brain behind the document "Defense Policy Guidance 1992-1994") as vice president and Donald Rumsfeld as secretary of defense made the dramatic swerve irreversible and the war inevitable.

Few events have changed the course of history as did the September 11th bombing of the Twin Towers in New York by a radical Muslim group. Obviously, the impact of that horrific tragedy reverberated differently with President Bush and his team. While the world was deeply saddened and in shock, the new administration vowed an apocalyptic revenge.

This was the final straw that ignited the fuse, setting the world in turmoil. However, two previous events had prepared the path to war. Both were related to George's father, Herbert Walker Bush, president from 1989 to 1993.

In his first inaugural address, George H. W. Bush expressed an optimistic view of the future:

> "I come before you and assume the Presidency at a moment rich with promise. For a new breeze is blowing, and a world refreshed by freedom seems reborn; for in man's heart, if not in fact, the day of the dictator is over. The totalitarian era is passing, its old ideas blown away like leaves from an ancient, lifeless tree. A new breeze is blowing, and a nation refreshed by freedom stands ready to push on. There is new ground to be broken and new action to be taken."

---

[15] See Part Two, Document 10.

However, despite this rosy picture of "the day of the dictator is over, he had to face the invasion of Kuwait by the brutal Iraqi dictator Saddam Hussein on August 1, 1990. Bush outperformed himself in rallying allies, international organizations, Congress, and the American people behind the U.S.-led coalition forces for the liberation of Kuwait. On January 17, 1991, a massive bombing took place with a ground invasion being launched on February 24. After a mere one hundred hours, the small, oil-rich nation was liberated and Bush made the decision to stop the offensive. His critics were furious because they wanted the total destruction of the Iraqi army, a march over Baghdad, and the overthrow of Saddam.

According to many, this big mistake needed to be corrected. However in retrospect, although the American ideologues of the "Project for the New American Century" would disagree, common sense folks can conclude that the father's decision not to overthrow the dictator was wiser than the son's determination to invade Iraq.

Another event that rekindled the ashes of war in the hawkish Pentagon strategists was the assassination attempt during the Clinton presidency on Bush Senior. Although no material evidence was ever found linking the so-called conspiracy to Iraq, conservative hardliners believed Clinton's response with some selective bombings was inadequate— almost wimpish.

Although never mentioned in any official documents, these two unfinished pieces of business had a considerable influence on Bush Junior's decision to go to war. In his eyes, Saddam needed to be taught a serious lesson: you shouldn't toy with America unless you're ready to pay a hefty price.

The social atmosphere that preceded and followed Bush's narrow margin victory in the 2000 presidential election might also have something to do with the Iraq invasion. Certainly in combination with the Twin Towers tragedy it can explain Americans' initial complacent attitude towards the war.

Although religious sentiments should be kept out of the political arena, as used to happen in the past, they played a considerable role here at home and abroad. Bush was put in power by a powerful conservative movement whose religious agenda coincides in many aspects of our social life with the right-wing political program. Religion and politics formed an impressive strategic alliance, reinforcing each other in the process. The result is an unsavory fanaticism that in the name of God is capable of justifying the most horrific actions. The war is one of them, welcomed by warmongers and religious zealots. The religious George Bush, wrapped in his conservative ideological cloak, would not find the idea of war repugnant.

Looking beyond our own backyard, more unsettling is the manifestations of religious fanaticism in the Arab world. To many, killing the enemy is a sacred mission that will be rewarded in heaven. Suicide bombers are the most twisted and shameful expressions of any religious faith.

This background of exalted religious faith and radical political ideology was the perfect humus that allowed the seeds planted by "Defense Policy Guidance 1992–1994" and "Rebuilding America's Defenses. Strategy, Forces and Resources for a New Century" (September 2000) to germinate vigorously. While Bill Clinton was attempting to present a real humanitarian and smarter America in a attractive vision of a superpower listening to the gripes of the poor and oppressed nations, Dick Cheney, Paul Wolfowitz, and Lewis Libby (just to mention a few) were formulating the concrete steps for America to exercise its leadership around the world.

The document "Rebuilding America's Defenses ..."[16] is a real revelation for many reasons. One stands out prominently. What our enemies have been saying all along of crude American imperialism is not only confirmed by this document, but is spelled out with graphic details. Both the letter and spirit of such a document were appropriated and implemented by George Bush with the deep conviction to carry out a noble mission of rescuing America from the abysm of ruin.

This is the real Bush Doctrine; this is his political bible. All the rest, so nicely stated in his inaugural addresses, speeches, and formal and informal conversations are mere smokescreens and common patriotic rhetoric to please people. The basic thesis of this document, repeatedly stated and emphasized, is that "the United States is the world's only superpower, combining preeminent military power, global technological leadership, and the world's largest economy."

According to this position, at present, the United States faced no global rival. America's grand strategy should be aimed at preserving

---

[16] Part Two, Document 10

and extending this advantageous position as far into the future as possible. Its mission was to exercise global leadership in order to preserve the present order and maintain the actual peace, "Pax Americana." Not to do so, would ultimately mean to throw the advantage away and face "greater threats, at higher costs and further risk to American lives" in the future. *Global leadership, preeminence,* and *dominant status* are the most common words used to describe the American imperialist role in the world. The document concludes that *America must match military means to geopolitical ends.*

The ninety-page document is a "road map for the nation's immediate and future defense plans." It states that a complete renovation of all the branches of the Armed Forces is needed in view of the "transformation of war made possible by new technologies" so as to preserve American preeminence. Today's task "is to secure and expand the *zones of democratic peace*; to deter the rise of a new great-power competitor; defend key regions of Europe, East Asia and the Middle East."

The Clinton Administration is often criticized in the document for cutting the defense budget, deferring defense investments, and creating a weapons procurement "bow wave" of immense proportions. Returning to the basic philosophy of preserving the American geopolitical leadership and the American global peace, the document advocates an increase in the military spending. This would procure a secure foundation for an unquestioned U.S. military preeminence.

Global supremacy can be achieved only through four essential missions. "None of the defense reviews of the past decade has weighed fully the range of missions demanded by U.S. global leadership," nor adequately quantified the forces and resources necessary to execute these missions successfully. These missions are: defending the homeland, fighting and winning multiple large-scale wars, conducting constabulary (police) missions that preserve the current peace, and transforming the U.S. armed forces to exploit the "revolution in military affairs."

To examine in detail the whole document would go beyond the scope of presenting a summarized version of the American Doctrine, but it would shed abundant light on this new vision of America. Just to get a taste of some of the views expressed in the document, consider a paragraph on nuclear arms and forces. In these few lines, the writers seem to deride the previous administrations:

> Whatever our fondest wishes the reality of today's world is that there is no magic wand with which to eliminate these weapons (or, more fundamentally, the interest in acquiring them) and that deterring their use requires a reliable and dominant U.S. nuclear capability.

Thus while the previous presidents worked hard at conventional and nuclear arms reduction, the Bush Administration believed that in order to maintain a political and military hegemony, it needed to increase and perfect its nuclear arsenal.

The document advocates a radical renovation and transformation of the armed forces who would assume new policing duties in space and cyberspace. Overall this new doctrine put forward by "a group of conservative interventionists" has a few tenets that constitute a revolutionary departure from the previous doctrines.

Here goes an interpretational and summarized reconstruction of this innovative doctrine as it transpires from the ninety-page document:

America is the sole global superpower (read, imperial power). As such, America is entrusted with special *responsibilities*, *duties*, and *rights*. One of its paramount responsibilities is to maintain the actual global order, and to preserve peace, the "Pax Americana." Among its fundamental duties, two excel for their ominous ramifications: to conduct constabulary missions of policing the planet, and to deter the rise of a new great-power competitor. The rights of an imperial power are unfettered and unrestrained, spanning from the right "to shape circumstances before crises emerge, and to meet threats before they become dire" to the unsolicited presence of American troops in every corner of the globe. Concretely, this means: to embrace pre-emptive attacks against perceived enemies; to ignore international opinion, international laws and organizations if that suits U.S. interests; and to establish military bases and stations on earth, in space, and under the sea. This in essence is the philosophy of the document that was embraced with fervor by Bush and militarily implemented after the September 11th terrorist attack with the invasion of Iraq.

Bush might not be original in his thinking, but he is certainly original in his decisions and with the people with whom he associates. Among the several factors previously mentioned, we don't really know what contributed the most to Bush's decision to invade Iraq. However, there's some certainty that the above-described doctrine had an impact with the September 11th attack being the final straw. At the risk of sounding irreverent, it could be said that the attack on the Twin Towers was the best gift ever bestowed by Osama bin Laden upon the Bush administration. Osama gave Bush on a silver platter the perfect reason to establish a permanent foothold in the heart of the Arab homeland. Ironically, bin Laden, whose terrorist acts have been so cheered and exalted by Muslim extremists around the world, provoked the catastrophe he always wanted to avoid: a U.S. military presence on Arab soil.

The hawkish strategists of the modern imperial doctrine secretly welcomed this chance of a lifetime. They didn't lose a second in exploiting the occasion for propaganda purposes. To justify the war, they cashed in on public outrage and fabricated a palatable reason for the invasion. The manipulation of public sentiments and opinion was masterful. Under the pretext of locating weapons of mass destruction (whose existence was never confirmed) and the noble idea of liberating the Iraqi people by a brutal dictator, the war was declared and the invasion of Iraq took place on March 20, 2003.

Finally, American troops were on Arab soil. Finally, the authors of the modern imperial doctrine had achieved their secret goal: to have a permanent foothold on that forbidden land, the land of oil and riches.

In this light, the withdrawal of the troops, the exit strategy, the violent hatred of Muslims towards America, the numerous losses of human lives, the international uproar and sentiments of hatred towards our great nation, etc. would not have any bearing on the Bush Administration's decisions. The higher the casualties caused by insurgents, suicide bombers, and religious sectarian factions, the better for justification for a continued American presence. The occupation will become permanent. This would sound totally heartless and cruel, but it is the unavoidable conclusion of this unusual doctrine, which is logical, coherent and realistic in its formulation and yet highly controversial in its premises. It is not surprising that nobody wants to mention it, not even in an election year.

However, the purpose of this discussion is not to criticize the authors of the doctrine or the Bush Administration for implementing it. On the contrary, their logic, realism, and determination should be admired in carrying on with similar antagonizing and divisive missions despite the general outcry and public pressure. What is deeply regrettable is the lack of transparency and the total absence of an honest debate on American foreign policy. Only a new administration with a very different philosophy and agenda or an unforeseen event of historical proportions can change the course of this American imperialist trend.

In the conclusion of the discussion of the Monroe doctrine, the question spontaneously arose, "Is this status of dominance and dependence spelled out unambiguously in any subsequent American Doctrine?" Now, we know the unequivocal answer to this unsettling question: George Bush, the man from Texas, unpretentious, unassuming, and with no special charisma or talent, has shaped a new, brazen America. Carter's obsession for human rights, Reagan and Weinberger's clear and precise guidelines, and Clinton's inspiring road map to a peaceful and prosperous twenty-first century have been swept away by a powerful new ideology, leaving behind a disfigured and tattered America for some, and for others, one that is powerful and feared.

CONCLUSION

From the concise exposition of the American Doctrine, transpires a diverse perception of the American role in the world. From Monroe to Bush, every interpretation has added its own characteristics and modalities. No doctrine is the exact replica of the previous one. However, despite some remarkable peculiarities, it is unquestionable that there is a substantial continuity linking all of them. Only George Bush's doctrine marks a radical departure from all the previous doctrines. His rupture with the past is so significant and dramatic that it can leave any scholar and historian in shock and awe.

Obviously, the conviction that the United States is a global empire with sole responsibility and authority of planetary policemen was not born with the Bush presidency. It is the culmination of a long process of several decades whose origins go beyond the "Defense Policy Guidance 1992–1994," ultimately getting lost in the mists of time. However, at its most simple, these two basic visions of America can be categorized as radically divergent from each other so as to occupy the opposite poles of any philosophical spectrum.

In the first vision (the traditional one), the face of America is fundamentally *humanitarian*, respectful, and generous, rooted in freedom and democracy even if tainted with global interventionist responsibilities.

In the second vision, (the new one), the face of America is categorically *imperial*, disrespectful of international conventions and laws, greedy, and rooted in planetary subjugation and domination.

Which vision is consistent with the values and aspirations of our Founding Fathers?

Which vision is consistent with the dynamics and laws of a world superpower?

Which one is idealistic and unattainable? Conversely, which one is realistic and inescapable?

The answers to these and many other questions might seem simple and straightforward on the surface, but deep down they present serious and seemingly unsolvable difficulties.

Let us end these reflections with a quote from the Gospel, in which Jesus appears to suggest a different exercise of power and authority among his disciples:

> You know that the rulers of the Gentiles lord it over them and the great ones make their authority over them felt. But it shall not be so among you. Rather, whoever whishes to be great among you shall be your servant; whoever whishes to be first among you shall be your slave.[17]

For Jesus there are two opposite types of authorities: one of the pagan (Gentile) rulers based on physical power and dominance, the other of his disciples based on service and humility.

Should there be an insurmountable difference between the secular power and the religious power, as suggested by Jesus? Alternatively, is it just a wishful thinking, an idealistic dream, with no possibility of realization, being both powers (secular and religious) exercised by humans?

Is it true that when we come to humans there is only one way to exercise power and authority, by imposition and coercion? Is it inescapable that even a benevolent tyrant will always be a tyrant?

Perhaps Jesus is not suggesting any concrete form of authority, whether religious or political. He may just be pointing out a new spirit that should inform any type of power. The concrete realizations can be multiple, but there should be only one spirit, that of service and humility. Jimmy Carter seems to be on the same wavelength – authority means to serve and not to be served.

Does this have any application in the realm of political theories?

Whatever the answer to this unsettling reality, a final thought that summarizes these reflections seems most fitting conclusion. From James Monroe to George W. Bush, America's historical journey has been amazing. From asserting as a young independent republic its right

---

[17] Matt. 20: 25–27. See The New American Bible, Catholic Bible Press, a division of Thomas Nelson Publishers, Nashville, 1979.

to be free from any intervention by foreign powers, America has ended up by proclaiming its right to intervene all over the globe. From a fledgling, attempting its first flight, America has now become a majestic eagle soaring over the earth.

The world belongs to America, and America does not belong to anybody.

DEFINITION OF DOCTRINE

After our astonishing and eye-opening journey into the "American Political Doctrine," it seems appropriate to formulate a definition that encapsulates the essence of this mystifying reality. Why do we need a radical new definition while many others are already out there? In all modesty, the ones examined so far have been so generic that they can barely be called definitions.

The Oxford English Dictionary[18] offers some helpful definitions:

That which is taught or laid down as true concerning a particular subject or department of knowledge, as religion, politics, science, etc.; a belief, theoretical opinion; a dogma, tenet.

In the most general sense: Instruction, teaching; a body of instruction or teaching.

A body or system of principles or tenets; a doctrinal or theoretical system; a theory; a science, or department of knowledge.

Monroe doctrine (U.S. politics): the name applied (since about 1848) to a principle or series of principles of policy put forward in, or deduced from, the Message of President Monroe to Congress, Dec. 2, 1823.

With no pretence to being an expert on the subject, and with no claim whatsoever to originality, I would suggest this definition:

The American Doctrine is a rational justification of a course of action, usually military in nature.

---

[18] Oxford English Dictionary online, Oxford University Press 2008.

In this definition, "course of action, usually military in nature" is a circumlocution for *war*. Thus the streamlined definition should be "The American Doctrine is a rational justification of war."

Yet however true, simple, transparent, or to the point, this definition presents insurmountable difficulties that might invalidate its substance. Everybody knows that war is unfortunately a constant and all-pervasive realty in our human history. We are dealing with an instrument that is supposed to solve conflicts *using military force rather than reason.* To accept this means to accept the law of the jungle in which the strongest and the fittest survive and triumph.

To be more specific, we are well aware that whoever wins a war is not necessarily the nation or person who is right. It is certainly the strongest and maybe the most cunning, but not necessarily the righteous one.

War is definitely an irrational instrument, which despite its constant use, acceptance, and justification, is totally inadequate to rightly solve human conflicts.

President Clinton was perfectly right when he said, "In over two hundred years of hard effort here at home, we have learned that the world works better *when differences are resolved by the force of argument rather than the force of arms.*"

In conclusion, to ascertain that there is a rational justification for something completely irrational is a paradox, a contradiction in terms, a total nonsense. Did we preempt and invalidate not only the definition of American Doctrine, but also the whole concept and reality behind it? Yet as long as there are people believing in it, and people formulating this doctrine, our assertions and conclusions lose any materiality or relevance, and thus fall on deaf ears.

DIVISION OF DOCTRINES

So far, we have dealt exclusively with the American political doctrine.

The two adjectives, *American* and *political,* narrow in such a way the vast area of so-called doctrine that we might lose the wider perspective of this reality.

For a better understanding, it would be beneficial to present a synopsis of what is considered doctrine if the term is interpreted as broadly as possible. Generally, this all-encompassing word *doctrine* refers to a vast array of realities that differ substantially and that have very specific claims. To simplify, there are two major doctrinal areas (religious and profane) that can be divided, for convenience purposes, into four specific groups.

First are all the *secular or profane* doctrines other than the American Doctrine. These are doctrines not connected with religion or holy things (e.g., doctrines regarding atoms, probability, gravitation, etc.)

Second are all the *religious* doctrines other than Catholicism. The division refers uniquely to the world of religions, like the Christian doctrine (the Lutheran doctrine, the Pentecostal doctrine, the Methodist doctrine…), the Muslim doctrine, the Hindu doctrine, etc.

Third is the Catholic doctrine. This is the doctrine presented by the Catholic Church with various and unique claims.

Finally, fourth is the American Doctrine (The exclusive subject of our investigation.) This deals uniquely with American political doctrine put forward by presidents such as Monroe and Bush.

The characteristics of each of these groups are quite peculiar and distinctive.

In the first group, the denomination "profane doctrine or scientific doctrine" can be easily interchanged with theory without losing anything of its original meaning. A secular doctrine can be true only if successfully tested by science.

In the second group, some of those religions, mainly Christians, present two fundamental claims. They claim to be of divine origin and to possess a uniqueness of truth. Every single one of these religions believes itself to be inspired directly by God and to be the only true religion. The rest of religions in this group do not stress those two characteristics, but believe in some divine origin and in some degree of exclusive truth.

The third group, Catholicism, constitutes a world in itself. It has fundamental claims unthinkable and unacceptable in the previous three.

Finally, in the fourth group consisting of the American Doctrine, the perception of its own essence varies radically from the previous groups. Here, there is no presumption of some divine origin or of some uniqueness of truth. There is no pretense of binding the mind and conscience of people. There is only an increasing awareness, in the conscience of its authors, that this doctrine is *licit*, *valid*, and *operative*. It is licit, because it is legal; valid, because it is acceptable and logical; and operative, because it is functional and effective.

The world must take notice of this doctrine, as the superpower will not hesitate to act upon it, whenever and however it deems it necessary.

Undoubtedly, the word *doctrine* contains a complex reality that can't be reduced to a simple definition. Whether those attributes that are made explicit in each of the four groups are true and essential has not been proven. The description given is a mere summary of what each group believes of itself and of its doctrine. However, in spite of this subjective approach, each description offers a valid instrument for understanding a reality that transcends simplifications and reductions.

CAN A DOCTRINE CHANGE?

It comes natural to think of a doctrine as something normative, stable, and lasting. Stability and durability gives credibility to any teaching, whether it is religious or political. Constant change in a doctrine would create confusion and uncertainty.

Let us now discuss two doctrines whose essence seems at odds with each other: the Catholic doctrine and the American Doctrine.

The Catholic Doctrine

The essence of the Catholic doctrine is *veridicity* (or *inherent truthfulness*) and *immutability*. Given these two basic components, any change would result in a contradiction or metaphysical impossibility. Being true and immutable, the doctrine remains the same through eternity.

The Catholic Church firmly believes that its doctrine is of divine origin. For this simple reason, it cannot be changed, altered, or modified in its essence. The modifications the doctrine has experienced through the centuries are only of form and not of substance. Developments of its contents are simple explications of what already was contained in the original nucleus of Revelation.

An example might better clarify this concept. As an apple seed develops into a beautiful tree, keeping invariable its essence through the different stages of its development, in the same way Catholic doctrine has developed its main core into an elaborate system of beliefs while keeping its substance intact.

The point of this discussion is not to prove or disprove whether this Catholic conviction is historically accurate, but only to stress its logic and coherence. Given the two basic components of the definition, veridicity or inherent truthfulness and immutability, there is no other possible posture than the one offered by the Catholic Church. As repository of the most venerable doctrine on earth, the Catholic Church is indubitably *mater et magistra* (mother and teacher) in this field. Moreover, the Catholic Church is convinced that it is the holder of the True Doctrine. No other organization or church can make a similar claim.

Returning for a moment to the *inherent truthfulness*, the Catholic Church firmly believes that its doctrine is the only *true doctrine*, positively excluding any other religion, because it *comes directly from God* through Divine Revelation. For this reason, it is immutable and eternal, allowing only development of truths already implicit in the original nucleus and rejecting any other addition or subtraction. All this is firmly anchored on the *infallibility of the Church* that cannot fail, according to Jesus's promise to Peter:

> And so I say to you, you are Peter, and upon this rock I will build my church and the gates of the netherworld shall not prevail against it. I will give you the keys to the kingdom of heaven. Whatever you bind on earth shall be bound in heaven; and whatever you loose on earth shall be loosed in heave.[19]

In another passage Jesus assures Peter of his unfailing support and assistance:

> Simon, Simon, behold Satan has demanded to sift all of you like wheat, but I have prayed that your own faith may not fail; and once you have turned back, you must strengthen your brothers.[20]

This uniqueness of the Catholic Church (divine origin and divine backing), makes it the exclusive source of salvation in the world, according to the unchallenged aphorism, *Extra Ecclesiam nulla salus* (outside the Church, there is no salvation).

The Catholic Church believes that its doctrine is immutable and true because of its divine origin and backing.

THE AMERICAN DOCTRINE

It would be a huge understatement to say that the American Doctrine does not have anything in common with the Catholic doctrine. Not only are they completely different, but they stand on the opposite extremes of that vast and undefined area called doctrine. Yet although both use the term *doctrine*, in reality they are antonyms and counter-figures of each other.

Unlike the Catholic doctrine that is of divine origin, the American Doctrine is of human origin.

Unlike the Catholic doctrine that possesses veridicity or inherent truthfulness and immutability, the American Doctrine does not claim any veridicity or immutability.

---

[19] Matt. 16: 18–19
[20] Luke 22: 31–32

The Catholic doctrine is compulsory and binding on its faithful, while the American Doctrine is neither compulsory nor binding. You can be a good American citizen without accepting the American Doctrine or believing in it. Conversely, you could not be a Catholic, much less a good Catholic, if you do not accept and believe in the Catholic doctrine.

Finally, the Catholic doctrine is concerned with souls and the heavenly kingdom, while the American Doctrine deals with bodies and the terrestrial empire.

This enumeration of differences could be dragged on ad infinitum, but the contrasts mentioned are sufficient to support the conclusion that an abyss of differences separates the two doctrines. At its heart, the American Doctrine is neither immutable nor eternal. It changes and adapts to historical circumstances.

Despite these insurmountable contrasts between these two doctrines, they seem to have at least one thing in common. Both are backed by the most awesome authority of the office.

No other power in the world can be compared to the American presidency and to the Catholic papacy. These two unlikely powers command respect and arouse fear, leaving no doubts of their effectiveness.

A final reflection seems inevitable. Does the American Doctrine provide a satisfying response to the aspirations of the majority of its citizens, or is it the product of a few aspiring to world domination? Is this the *real American dream*—or its worst nightmare?

These questions are not being asked for the simple pleasure of posing them, but with the intention to promote a serious reflection on the American Doctrine and all its implications. If this goal can be reached without anyone being judged or prejudged, and with everybody's ideas being respected, the mission will be accomplished. *This mission is to reflect (hence the heading "Reflections for Beginners") in order for us to be more aware of the complex and seemingly inextricable reality we are living in and be able to attempt some feasible transformation.*

SECOND PART

DOCUMENTATION FOR "THE AMERICAN DOCTRINE"[21]

---

[21] All the documents in this second part are from various internet websites. Among the many websites, only one will be cited for each document.
For the Monroe Doctrine, See Avalon Project at Yale Law School on line: www.**yale.edu**/lawweb/avalon/**monroe**.htm

1
THE MONROE DOCTRINE

The Monroe Doctrine was expressed during President Monroe's seventh annual message to Congress on December 2, 1823. The text is as follows:

. . . At the proposal of the Russian Imperial Government, made through the minister of the Emperor residing here, a full power and instructions have been transmitted to the minister of the United States at St. Petersburg to arrange by amicable negotiation the respective rights and interests of the two nations on the northwest coast of this continent. A similar proposal has been made by His Imperial Majesty to the Government of Great Britain, which has likewise been acceded to. The Government of the United States has been desirous by this friendly proceeding of manifesting the great value which they have invariably attached to the friendship of the Emperor and their solicitude to cultivate the best understanding with his Government. In the discussions to which this interest has given rise and in the arrangements by which they may terminate the occasion has been judged proper for asserting, as a principle in which the rights and interests of the United States are involved, that the American continents, by the free and independent condition which they have assumed and maintain, are henceforth not to be considered as subjects for future colonization by any European powers....

It was stated at the commencement of the last session that a great effort was then making in Spain and Portugal to improve the condition of the people of those countries, and that it appeared to be conducted with extraordinary moderation. It need scarcely be remarked that the results have been so far very different from what was then anticipated. Of events in that quarter of the globe, with which we have so much intercourse and from which we derive our origin, we have always been anxious and interested spectators. The citizens of the United States cherish sentiments the most friendly in favor of the liberty and happiness of their fellow-men on that side of the Atlantic. In the wars of the European powers in matters relating to themselves we have never taken any part, nor does it comport with our policy to do so. It is only when our rights are invaded or seriously menaced that we resent injuries or make preparation for our defense. With the movements in this hemisphere we are of necessity more immediately connected, and by causes which must be obvious to all enlightened and impartial observers. The political system of the allied powers is essentially different in this respect from that of America. This difference proceeds from that which exists in their respective Governments; and to the defense of our own, which has been achieved by the loss of so much blood and treasure, and matured by the wisdom of their most enlightened citizens, and under which we have enjoyed unexampled felicity, this whole nation is devoted. We owe it, therefore, to candor and to the amicable relations existing between the United States and those powers to declare that we should consider any attempt on their part to extend their system to any portion of this hemisphere as dangerous to our peace and safety. With the existing colonies or dependencies of any European power we have not interfered and shall not interfere. But with the Governments who have declared their independence and maintain it, and whose independence we have, on great consideration and on just principles, acknowledged, we could not view any interposition for the purpose of oppressing them, or controlling in any other manner their destiny, by any European power in any other light than as the manifestation of an unfriendly disposition toward the United States. In the war between those new Governments and Spain we declared our neutrality at the time of their recognition, and to this we have adhered, and shall continue to adhere, provided no change shall occur which, in the judgement of the competent authorities of this Government, shall make a corresponding change on the part of the United States indispensable to their security.

The late events in Spain and Portugal shew that Europe is still unsettled. Of this important fact no stronger proof can be adduced than that the allied powers should have thought it proper, on any principle satisfactory to themselves, to have interposed by force in the internal concerns of Spain. To what extent such interposition may be carried, on the same principle, is a question in which all independent powers whose governments differ from theirs are interested, even those most remote, and surely none of them more so than the United States. Our policy in regard to Europe, which was adopted at an early stage of the wars which have so long agitated that quarter of the globe, nevertheless remains the same, which is, not to interfere in the internal concerns of any of its powers; to consider the government de facto as the legitimate government for us; to cultivate friendly relations with it, and to preserve those relations by a frank, firm, and manly policy, meeting in all instances the just claims of every power, submitting to injuries from none. But in regard to those continents circumstances are eminently and conspicuously different.

It is impossible that the allied powers should extend their political system to any portion of either continent without endangering our peace and happiness; nor can anyone believe that our southern brethren, if left to themselves, would adopt it of their own accord. It is equally impossible, therefore, that we should behold such interposition in any form with indifference. If we look to the comparative strength and resources of Spain and those new Governments, and their distance from each other, it must be obvious that she can never subdue them. It is still the true policy of the United States to leave the parties to themselves, in hope that other powers will pursue the same course....

2
THEODORE ROOSEVELT'S COROLLARY TO THE MONROE DOCTRINE[22]

Annual Message to Congress, December 6, 1904

FOREIGN POLICY

In treating of our foreign policy and of the attitude that this great Nation should assume in the world at large, it is absolutely necessary to consider the Army and the Navy, and the Congress, through which the thought of the Nation finds its expression, should keep ever vividly in mind the fundamental fact that it is impossible to treat our foreign policy, whether this policy takes shape in the effort to secure justice for others or justice for ourselves, save as conditioned upon the attitude we are willing to take toward our Army, and especially toward our Navy. It is not merely unwise, it is contemptible, for a nation, as for an individual, to use high-sounding language to proclaim its purposes, or to take positions which are ridiculous if unsupported by potential force, and then to refuse to provide this force. If there is no intention of

---

[22] www.**ourdocuments.gov**/doc.php?doc=56&page=transcript

providing and keeping the force necessary to back up a strong attitude, then it is far better not to assume such an attitude.

The steady aim of this Nation, as of all enlightened nations, should be to strive to bring ever nearer the day when there shall prevail throughout the world the peace of justice. There are kinds of peace which are highly undesirable, which are in the long run as destructive as any war. Tyrants and oppressors have many times made a wilderness and called it peace. Many times peoples who were slothful or timid or shortsighted, who had been enervated by ease or by luxury, or misled by false teachings, have shrunk in unmanly fashion from doing duty that was stern and that needed self-sacrifice, and have sought to hide from their own minds their shortcomings, their ignoble motives, by calling them love of peace. The peace of tyrannous terror, the peace of craven weakness, the peace of injustice, all these should be shunned as we shun unrighteous war. The goal to set before us as a nation, the goal which should be set before all mankind, is the attainment of the peace of justice, of the peace which comes when each nation is not merely safe-guarded in its own rights, but scrupulously recognizes and performs its duty toward others. Generally peace tells for righteousness; but if there is conflict between the two, then our fealty is due first to the cause of righteousness. Unrighteous wars are common, and unrighteous peace is rare; but both should be shunned. The right of freedom and the responsibility for the exercise of that right can not be divorced. One of our great poets has well and finely said that freedom is not a gift that tarries long in the hands of cowards. Neither does it tarry long in the hands of those too slothful, too dishonest, or too unintelligent to exercise it. The eternal vigilance which is the price of liberty must be exercised, sometimes to guard against outside foes; although of course far more often to guard against our own selfish or thoughtless shortcomings.

If these self-evident truths are kept before us, and only if they are so kept before us, we shall have a clear idea of what our foreign policy in its larger aspects should be. It is our duty to remember that a nation has no more right to do injustice to another nation, strong or weak, than an individual has to do injustice to another individual; that the same moral law applies in one case as in the other. But we must also remember that it is as much the duty of the Nation to guard its own rights and its own interests as it is the duty of the individual so to do.

Within the Nation the individual has now delegated this right to the State, that is, to the representative of all the individuals, and it is a maxim of the law that for every wrong there is a remedy. But in international law we have not advanced by any means as far as we have advanced in municipal law. There is as yet no judicial way of enforcing a right in international law. When one nation wrongs another or wrongs many others, there is no tribunal before which the wrongdoer can be brought. Either it is necessary supinely to acquiesce in the wrong, and thus put a premium upon brutality and aggression, or else it is necessary for the aggrieved nation valiantly to stand up for its rights. Until some method is devised by which there shall be a degree of international control over offending nations, it would be a wicked thing for the most civilized powers, for those with most sense of international obligations and with keenest and most generous appreciation of the difference between right and wrong, to disarm. If the great civilized nations of the present day should completely disarm, the result would mean an immediate recrudescence of barbarism in one form or another. Under any circumstances a sufficient armament would have to be kept up to serve the purposes of international police; and until international cohesion and the sense of international duties and rights are far more advanced than at present, a nation desirous both of securing respect for itself and of doing good to others must have a force adequate for the work which it feels is allotted to it as its part of the general world duty. Therefore it follows that a self-respecting, just, and far-seeing nation should on the one hand endeavor by every means to aid in the development of the various movements which tend to provide substitutes for war, which tend to render nations in their actions toward one another, and indeed toward their own peoples, more responsive to the general sentiment of humane and civilized mankind; and on the other hand that it should keep prepared, while scrupulously avoiding wrongdoing itself, to repel any wrong, and in exceptional cases to take action which in a more advanced stage of international relations would come under the head of the exercise of the international police. A great free people owes it to itself and to all mankind not to sink into helplessness before the powers of evil.

ARBITRATION TREATIES—SECOND HAGUE CONFERENCE

We are in every way endeavoring to help on, with cordial good will, every movement which will tend to bring us into more friendly relations with the rest of mankind. In pursuance of this policy I shall shortly lay before the Senate treaties of arbitration with all powers which are willing to enter into these treaties with us. It is not possible at this period of the world's development to agree to arbitrate all matters, but there are many matters of possible difference between us and other nations which can be thus arbitrated. Furthermore, at the request of the Interparliamentary Union, an eminent body composed of practical statesmen from all countries, I have asked the Powers to join with this Government in a second Hague conference, at which it is hoped that the work already so happily begun at The Hague may be carried some steps further toward completion. This carries out the desire expressed by the first Hague conference itself.

POLICY TOWARD OTHER NATIONS OF THE WESTERN HEMISPHERE

It is not true that the United States feels any land hunger or entertains any projects as regards the other nations of the Western Hemisphere save such as are for their welfare. All that this country desires is to see the neighboring countries stable, orderly, and prosperous. Any country whose people conduct themselves well can count upon our hearty friendship. If a nation shows that it knows how to act with reasonable efficiency and decency in social and political matters, if it keeps order and pays its obligations, it need fear no interference from the United States. *Chronic wrongdoing, or an impotence which results in a general loosening of the ties of civilized society, may in America, as elsewhere, ultimately require intervention by some civilized nation, and in the Western Hemisphere the adherence of the United States to the Monroe Doctrine may force the United States, however reluctantly, in flagrant cases of such wrongdoing or impotence, to the exercise of an international police power.* If every country washed by the Caribbean Sea would show the progress in stable and just civilization which with the aid of the Platt Amendment Cuba has shown since our troops left the island, and which so many of the republics in both Americas are constantly and brilliantly showing, all question of interference by this Nation with their affairs would be at an end. Our interests and those of our southern neighbors are in reality identical. They have great natural riches, and if within their borders the reign of law and justice obtains, prosperity is sure to come to them. While they thus obey the primary laws of civilized society they may rest assured that they will be treated by us in a spirit of cordial and helpful sympathy. *We would interfere with them only in the last resort, and then only if it became evident that their inability or unwillingness to do justice at home and abroad had violated the rights of the United States or had invited foreign aggression to the detriment of the entire body of American nations.* It is a mere truism to say that every nation, whether in America or anywhere else, which desires to maintain its freedom, its independence, must ultimately realize that the right of such independence can not be separated from the responsibility of making good use of it.

In asserting the Monroe Doctrine, in taking such steps as we have taken in regard to Cuba, Venezuela, and Panama, and in endeavoring to circumscribe the theater of war in the Far East, and to secure the open door in China, we have acted in our own interest as well as in the interest of humanity at large. There are, however, cases in which, while our own interests are not greatly involved, strong appeal is made to our sympathies. Ordinarily it is very much wiser and more useful for us to concern ourselves with striving for our own moral and material betterment here at home than to concern ourselves with trying to better the condition of things in other nations. We have plenty of sins of our own to war against, and under ordinary circumstances we can do more for the general uplifting of humanity by striving with heart and soul to put a stop to civic corruption, to brutal lawlessness and violent race prejudices here at home than by passing resolutions and wrongdoing elsewhere. Nevertheless there are occasional crimes committed on so vast a scale and of such peculiar horror as to make us doubt whether it is not our manifest duty to endeavor at least to show our disapproval of the deed and our sympathy with those who have suffered by it. The cases must be extreme in which such a course is justifiable. There must be no effort made to remove the mote from our brother's eye if we refuse to remove the beam from our own. But in extreme cases action may be justifiable and proper. What form the action shall take must depend upon the circumstances of the case; that is, upon the degree of the atrocity and upon our power to remedy it. The cases in which we could interfere by force of arms as we interfered to put a stop to intolerable conditions in Cuba are necessarily very few. Yet it is not to be expected that a people like ours, which in spite of certain very obvious shortcomings, nevertheless as a whole shows by its consistent practice its belief in the principles of civil and religious liberty and of orderly freedom, a people among whom even the worst crime, like the crime of lynching, is never more than sporadic, so that individuals and not classes are molested in their fundamental rights—it is inevitable that such a nation should desire eagerly to give expression to its horror on an occasion like that of the massacre of the Jews in Kishenef, or when it witnesses such systematic and long-extended cruelty and oppression as the cruelty and oppression of which the Armenians have been the victims, and which have won for them the indignant pity of the civilized world.

3
HENRY CABOT LODGE: COROLLARY TO THE MONROE DOCTRINE [23]

Source: *Record,* 62 Cong., 2 Sess., p. 10045.

Resolved, that when any harbor or other place in the American continents is so situated that the occupation thereof for naval or military purposes might threaten the communications or the safety of the United States, the government of the United States could not see without grave concern the possession of such harbor or other place by any corporation or association which has such a relation to another government, not American, as to give that government practical power of control for national purposes. . . .

This resolution rests on a generally accepted principle of the law of nations, older than the Monroe Doctrine. It rests on the principle that every nation has a right to protect its own safety, and that if it feels that the possession by a foreign power, for military or naval purposes, of any given harbor or place is prejudicial to its safety, it is its duty as well as its right to interfere.

---

[23] www.**mtholyoke.edu**/acad/intrel/lodge2.htm

I will instance as an example of what I mean the protest that was made successfully against the occupation of the port of Agadir, in Morocco, by Germany. England objected on the ground that it threatened her communication through the Mediterranean. That view was shared largely by the European powers, and the occupation of that port was prevented in that way. That is the principle upon which the resolution rests.

It has been made necessary by a change of modern conditions, under which, while a government takes no action itself, the possession of an important place of the character I have described may be taken by a corporation or association which would be under the control of the foreign government.

The Monroe Doctrine was, of course, an extension in our own interests of this underlying principle—the right of every nation to provide for its own safety. The Monroe Doctrine, as we all know, was applied, so far as the taking possession of territory was concerned, to its being open to further colonization and naturally did not touch upon the precise point involved here. But without any Monroe Doctrine, the possession of a harbor such as that of Magdalena Bay, which has led to this resolution would render it necessary, I think, to make some declaration covering a case where corporation or association was involved.

In this particular case it became apparent from the inquiries made by the committee and by the administration that no government was concerned in taking possession of Magdalena Bay; but it also became apparent that those persons who held control of the Mexican concession, which included the land about Magdalena Bay, were engaged in negotiations, which have not yet been completed certainly but which have only been tentative, looking to the sale of that bay and the land about it to a corporation either created or authorized by a foreign government or in which the stock was largely held or controlled by foreigners.

The passage of this resolution has seemed to the committee, without division, I think, to be in the interest of peace. It is always desirable to make the position of a country in regard to a question of this kind known beforehand and not to allow a situation to arise in which it might be necessary to urge a friendly power to withdraw when that withdrawal could not be made, perhaps, without some humiliation.

The resolution is merely a statement of policy, allied to the Monroe Doctrine, of course, but not necessarily dependent upon it or growing out of it. When the message came in, I made a statement as to the conditions at Magdalena Bay which had led to the resolution of inquiry and which has now led to the subsequent action of the committee. It seemed to the committee that it was very wise to make this statement of policy at this time, when it can give offense to no one and makes the position of the United States clear.

Of course I need not say to the Senate that the opening of the Panama Canal gives to the question of Magdalena Bay and to that of the Galapagos Islands, which have been once or twice before considered, an importance such as they have never possessed, and I think it eminently desirable in every interest that this resolution should receive the assent of the Senate.

4

TRUMAN DOCTRINE[24]

Harry S Truman
Address before a joint session of Congress on March 12, 1947

Mr. President, Mr. Speaker, Members of the Congress of the United States:

The gravity of the situation which confronts the world today necessitates my appearance before a joint session of the Congress. The foreign policy and the national security of this country are involved.

One aspect of the present situation, which I wish to present to you at this time for your consideration and decision, concerns Greece and Turkey.

The United States has received from the Greek Government an urgent appeal for financial and economic assistance. Preliminary reports from the American Economic Mission now in Greece and reports from the American Ambassador in Greece corroborate the statement of the Greek Government that assistance is imperative if Greece is to survive as a free nation.

I do not believe that the American people and the Congress wish to turn a deaf ear to the appeal of the Greek Government.

---

[24] www.**ahistoryofgreece.com**/trumandoctrine.htm

Greece is not a rich country. Lack of sufficient natural resources has always forced the Greek people to work hard to make both ends meet. Since 1940, this industrious and peace loving country has suffered invasion, four years of cruel enemy occupation, and bitter internal strife.

When forces of liberation entered Greece they found that the retreating Germans had destroyed virtually all the railways, roads, port facilities, communications, and merchant marine. More than a thousand villages had been burned. Eighty-five percent of the children were tubercular. Livestock, poultry, and draft animals had almost disappeared. Inflation had wiped out practically all savings.

As a result of these tragic conditions, a militant minority, exploiting human want and misery, was able to create political chaos which, until now, has made economic recovery impossible.

Greece is today without funds to finance the importation of those goods which are essential to bare subsistence. Under these circumstances the people of Greece cannot make progress in solving their problems of reconstruction. Greece is in desperate need of financial and economic assistance to enable it to resume purchases of food, clothing, fuel and seeds. These are indispensable for the subsistence of its people and are obtainable only from abroad. Greece must have help to import the goods necessary to restore internal order and security, so essential for economic and political recovery.

The Greek Government has also asked for the assistance of experienced American administrators, economists and technicians to insure that the financial and other aid given to Greece shall be used effectively in creating a stable and self-sustaining economy and in improving its public administration.

The very existence of the Greek state is today threatened by the terrorist activities of several thousand armed men, led by Communists, who defy the government's authority at a number of points, particularly along the northern boundaries. A Commission appointed by the United Nations security Council is at present investigating disturbed conditions in northern Greece and alleged border violations along the frontier between Greece on the one hand and Albania, Bulgaria, and Yugoslavia on the other.

Meanwhile, the Greek Government is unable to cope with the situation. The Greek army is small and poorly equipped. It needs supplies and equipment if it is to restore the authority of the government throughout Greek territory. Greece must have assistance if it is to become a self-supporting and self-respecting democracy.

The United States must supply that assistance. We have already extended to Greece certain types of relief and economic aid but these are inadequate.

There is no other country to which democratic Greece can turn.

No other nation is willing and able to provide the necessary support for a democratic Greek government.

The British Government, which has been helping Greece, can give no further financial or economic aid after March 31. Great Britain finds itself under the necessity of reducing or liquidating its commitments in several parts of the world, including Greece.

We have considered how the United Nations might assist in this crisis. But the situation is an urgent one requiring immediate action and the United Nations and its related organizations are not in a position to extend help of the kind that is required.

It is important to note that the Greek Government has asked for our aid in utilizing effectively the financial and other assistance we may give to Greece, and in improving its public administration. It is of the utmost importance that we supervise the use of any funds made available to Greece; in such a manner that each dollar spent will count toward making Greece self-supporting, and will help to build an economy in which a healthy democracy can flourish.

No government is perfect. One of the chief virtues of a democracy, however, is that its defects are always visible and under democratic processes can be pointed out and corrected. The Government of Greece is not perfect. Nevertheless it represents eighty-five per cent of the members of the Greek Parliament who were chosen in an election last year. Foreign observers, including 692 Americans, considered this election to be a fair expression of the views of the Greek people.

The Greek Government has been operating in an atmosphere of chaos and extremism. It has made mistakes. The extension of aid by this country does not mean that the United States condones everything that the Greek Government has done or will do. We have condemned in the past, and we condemn now, extremist measures of the right or the left. We have in the past advised tolerance, and we advise tolerance now.

Greece's neighbor, Turkey, also deserves our attention.

The future of Turkey as an independent and economically sound state is clearly no less important to the freedom-loving peoples of the world than the future of Greece. The circumstances in which Turkey finds itself today are considerably different from those of Greece. Turkey has been spared the disasters that have beset Greece. And during the war, the United States and Great Britain furnished Turkey with material aid.

Nevertheless, Turkey now needs our support.

Since the war Turkey has sought financial assistance from Great Britain and the United States for the purpose of effecting that modernization necessary for the maintenance of its national integrity.

That integrity is essential to the preservation of order in the Middle East.

The British government has informed us that, owing to its own difficulties can no longer extend financial or economic aid to Turkey.

As in the case of Greece, if Turkey is to have the assistance it needs, the United States must supply it. We are the only country able to provide that help.

I am fully aware of the broad implications involved if the United States extends assistance to Greece and Turkey, and I shall discuss these implications with you at this time.

One of the primary objectives of the foreign policy of the United States is the creation of conditions in which we and other nations will be able to work out a way of life free from coercion. This was a fundamental issue in the war with Germany and Japan. Our victory was won over countries which sought to impose their will, and their way of life, upon other nations.

To ensure the peaceful development of nations, free from coercion, the United States has taken a leading part in establishing the United Nations. The United Nations is designed to make possible lasting freedom and independence for all its members. We shall not realize our objectives, however, unless we are willing to help free peoples to maintain their free institutions and their national integrity against aggressive movements that seek to impose upon them totalitarian regimes. This is no more than a frank recognition that totalitarian regimes imposed on free peoples, by direct or indirect aggression, undermine the foundations of international peace and hence the security of the United States.

The peoples of a number of countries of the world have recently had totalitarian regimes forced upon them against their will. The Government of the United States has made frequent protests against coercion and intimidation, in violation of the Yalta agreement, in Poland, Rumania, and Bulgaria. I must also state that in a number of other countries there have been similar developments.

At the present moment in world history nearly every nation must choose between alternative ways of life. The choice is too often not a free one.

One way of life is based upon the will of the majority, and is distinguished by free institutions, representative government, free elections, guarantees of individual liberty, freedom of speech and religion, and freedom from political oppression.

The second way of life is based upon the will of a minority forcibly imposed upon the majority. It relies upon terror and oppression, a controlled press and radio, fixed elections, and the suppression of personal freedoms.

I believe that it must be the policy of the United States to support free peoples who are resisting attempted subjugation by armed minorities or by outside pressures.

I believe that we must assist free peoples to work out their own destinies in their own way.

I believe that our help should be primarily through economic and financial aid which is essential to economic stability and orderly political processes.

The world is not static, and the status quo is not sacred. But we cannot allow changes in the status quo in violation of the Charter of the United Nations by such methods as coercion, or by such subterfuges as political infiltration. In helping free and independent nations to maintain their freedom, the United States will be giving effect to the principles of the Charter of the United Nations.

It is necessary only to glance at a map to realize that the survival and integrity of the Greek nation are of grave importance in a much wider situation. If Greece should fall under the control of an armed minority, the effect upon its neighbor, Turkey, would be immediate and serious. Confusion and disorder might well spread throughout the entire Middle East.

Moreover, the disappearance of Greece as an independent state would have a profound effect upon those countries in Europe whose peoples are struggling against great difficulties to maintain their freedoms and their independence while they repair the damages of war.

It would be an unspeakable tragedy if these countries, which have struggled so long against overwhelming odds, should lose that victory for which they sacrificed so much. Collapse of free institutions and loss of independence would be disastrous not only for them but for the world. Discouragement and possibly failure would quickly be the lot of neighboring peoples striving to maintain their freedom and independence.

Should we fail to aid Greece and Turkey in this fateful hour, the effect will be far reaching to the West as well as to the East.

We must take immediate and resolute action.

I therefore ask the Congress to provide authority for assistance to Greece and Turkey in the amount of $400,000,000 for the period ending June 30, 1948. In requesting these funds, I have taken into consideration the maximum amount of relief assistance which would be furnished to Greece out of the $350,000,000 which I recently requested that the Congress authorize for the prevention of starvation and suffering in countries devastated by the war.

In addition to funds, I ask the Congress to authorize the detail of American civilian and military personnel to Greece and Turkey, at the request of those countries, to assist in the tasks of reconstruction, and for the purpose of supervising the use of such financial and material assistance as may be furnished. I recommend that authority also be provided for the instruction and training of selected Greek and Turkish personnel.

Finally, I ask that the Congress provide authority which will permit the speediest and most effective use, in terms of needed commodities, supplies, and equipment, of such funds as may be authorized.

If further funds, or further authority, should be needed for purposes indicated in this message, I shall not hesitate to bring the situation before the Congress. On this subject the Executive and Legislative branches of the Government must work together.

This is a serious course upon which we embark.

I would not recommend it except that the alternative is much more serious. The United States contributed $341,000,000,000 toward winning World War II. This is an investment in world freedom and world peace.

The assistance that I am recommending for Greece and Turkey amounts to little more than 1 tenth of 1 per cent of this investment. It is only common sense that we should safeguard this investment and make sure that it was not in vain.

The seeds of totalitarian regimes are nurtured by misery and want. They spread and grow in the evil soil of poverty and strife. They reach their full growth when the hope of a people for a better life has died. We must keep that hope alive.

The free peoples of the world look to us for support in maintaining their freedoms.

If we falter in our leadership, we may endanger the peace of the world—and we shall surely endanger the welfare of our own nation.

Great responsibilities have been placed upon us by the swift movement of events.

I am confident that the Congress will face these responsibilities squarely.

5

PRESIDENT NIXON'S SPEECH ON *VIETNAMIZATION*

November 3, 1969.[25]

Good evening, my fellow Americans:
Tonight I want to talk to you on a subject of deep concern to all Americans and to many people in all parts of the world the war in Vietnam.

I believe that one of the reasons for the deep division about Vietnam is that many Americans have lost confidence in what their Government has told them about our policy. The American people cannot and should not be asked to support a policy which involves the overriding issues of war and peace unless they know the truth about that policy.

Tonight, therefore, I would like to answer some of the questions that I know are on the minds of many of you listening to me. How and why did America get involved in Vietnam in the first place? How has this administration changed the policy of the previous administration?

---

[25] www.**famousquotes.me.uk/speeches**/Richard_**Nixon**/2.htm

What has really happened in the negotiations in Paris and on the battlefront in Vietnam? What choices do we have if we are to end the war? What are the prospects for peace?

Now, let me begin by describing the situation I found when I was inaugurated on January 20.

—The war had been going on for 4 years.

—31,000 Americans had been killed in action.

—The training program for the South Vietnamese was behind schedule.

—540,000 Americans were in Vietnam with no plans to reduce the number.

—No progress had been made at the negotiations in Paris and the United States had not put forth a comprehensive peace proposal.

—The war was causing deep division at home and criticism from many of our friends as well as our enemies abroad. In view of these circumstances there were some who urged that I end the war at once by ordering the immediate withdrawal of all American forces.

From a political standpoint this would have been a popular and easy course to follow. After all, we became involved in the war while my predecessor was in office. I could blame the defeat which would be the result of my action on him and come out as the peacemaker. Some put it to me quite bluntly: This was the only way to avoid allowing Johnson's war to become Nixon's war. But I had a greater obligation than to think only of the years of my administration and of the next election. I had to think of the effect of my decision on the next generation and on the future of peace and freedom in America and in the world.

Let us all understand that the question before us is not whether some Americans are for peace and some Americans are against peace. The question at issue is not whether Johnson's war becomes Nixon's war.

The great question is: How can we win America's peace?

Well, let us turn now to the fundamental issue. Why and how did the United States become involved in Vietnam in the first place?

Fifteen years ago North Vietnam, with the logistical support of Communist China and the Soviet Union, launched a campaign to impose a Communist government on South Vietnam by instigating and supporting a revolution.

In response to the request of the Government of South Vietnam, President Eisenhower sent economic aid and military equipment to assist the people of South Vietnam in their efforts to prevent a Communist takeover. Seven years ago, President Kennedy sent sixteen thousand military personnel to Vietnam as combat advisers. Four years ago, President Johnson sent American combat forces to South Vietnam.

Now, many believe that President Johnson's decision to send American combat forces to South Vietnam was wrong. Any many others I among them have been strongly critical of the way the war has been conducted.

But the question facing us today is: Now that we are in the war, what is the best way to end it? In January I could only conclude that the precipitate withdrawal of American forces from Vietnam would be a disaster not only for South Vietnam but for the United States and for the cause of peace. For the South Vietnamese, our precipitate withdrawal would inevitably allow the Communists to repeat the massacres which followed their takeover in the North fifteen years before.

—They then murdered more than fifty thousand people and hundreds of thousands more died in slave labor camps.

—We saw a prelude of what would happen in South Vietnam when the Communists entered the city of Hue last year. During their brief rule there, there was a bloody reign of terror in which three thousand civilians were clubbed, shot to death, and buried in mass graves.

—With the sudden collapse of our support, these atrocities of Hue would become the nightmare of the entire nation and particularly for the million and a half Catholic refugees who fled to South Vietnam when the Communists took over in the North.

For the United States, this first defeat in our Nation's history would result in a collapse of confidence in American leadership, not only in Asia but through-out the world. Three American Presidents have recognized the great stakes involved in Vietnam and understood what had to be done.

In 1963, President Kennedy, with his characteristic eloquence and clarity, said: "... we want to see a stable government there, carrying on a struggle to maintain its national independence.

"We believe strongly in that. We are not going to withdraw from that effort. In my opinion, for us to withdraw from that effort would mean a collapse not only of South Vietnam, but Southeast Asia. So we are going to stay there.

"President Eisenhower and President Johnson expressed the same conclusion during their terms of office. For the future of peace, precipitate withdrawal would thus be a disaster of immense magnitude.

—A nation cannot remain great if it betrays its allies and lets down its friends.

—Our defeat and humiliation in South Vietnam without question would promote recklessness in the councils of those great powers who have not yet abandoned their goals of world conquest.

—This would spark violence wherever our commitments help maintain the peace in the Middle East, in Berlin, eventually even in the Western Hemisphere. Ultimately, this would cost more lives. It would not bring peace; it would bring more war.

For these reasons, I rejected the recommendation that I should end the war by immediately withdrawing all of our forces. I chose instead to change American policy on both the negotiating front and battlefront....We Americans are a do-it-yourself people. We are an impatient people.

Instead of teaching someone else to do a job, we like to do it ourselves. And this trait has been carried over into our foreign policy.

In Korea and again in Vietnam, the United States furnished most of the money, most of the arms, and most of the men to help the people of those countries defend their freedom against Communist aggression. Before any American troops were committed to Vietnam, a leader of another Asian country expressed this opinion to me when I was traveling in Asia as a private citizen. He said: "When you are trying to assist another nation defend its freedom, U.S. policy should be to help them fight the war but not to fight the war for them." ... Well, in accordance with this wise counsel, I laid down in Guam three principles as guidelines for future American policy toward Asia:

—First, the United States will keep all of its treaty commitments.

—Second, we shall provide a shield if a nuclear power threatens the freedom of a nation allied with us or of a nation whose survival we consider vital to our security.

—Third, in cases involving other types of aggression, we shall furnish military and economic assistance when requested in accordance with our treaty commitments. But we shall look to the nation directly threatened to assume the primary responsibility of providing the manpower for its defense. After I announced this policy, I found that the leaders of the Philippines, Thailand, Vietnam, South Korea, and other nations which might be threatened by Communist aggression, welcomed this new direction in American foreign policy.

The defense of freedom is everybody's business not just America's business. And it is particularly the responsibility of the people whose freedom is threatened. In the previous administration, we Americanized the war in Vietnam. In this administration, we are Vietnamizing the search for peace.

The policy of the previous administration not only resulted in our assuming the primary responsibility for fighting the war, but even more significantly did not adequately stress the goal of strengthening the South Vietnamese so that they could defend themselves when we left.

The Vietnamization plan was launched following Secretary Laird's visit to Vietnam in March. Under the plan, I ordered first a substantial increase in the training and equipment of South Vietnamese forces.

—After five years of Americans going into Vietnam, we are finally bringing men home. By December 15, over sixty thousand men will have been withdrawn from South Vietnam including 20 percent of all of our combat forces.

—The South Vietnamese have continued to gain in strength. As a result they have been able to take over combat responsibilities from our American troops.

Two other significant developments have occurred since this administration took office.

—Enemy infiltration, infiltration which is essential if they are to launch a major attack, over the last three months is less than 20 percent of what it was over the same period last year.

—Most important United States casualties have declined during the last two months to the lowest point in three years.

Let me now turn to our program for the future. We have adopted a plan which we have worked out in cooperation with the South Vietnamese for the complete withdrawal of all U.S. combat ground forces, and their replacement by South Vietnamese forces on an orderly scheduled timetable. This withdrawal will be made from strength and not from weakness. As South Vietnamese forces become stronger, the rate of American withdrawal can become greater.

I have not and do not intend to announce the timetable for our program. And there are obvious reasons for this decision which I am sure you will understand. As I have indicated on several occasions, the rate of withdrawal will depend on developments on three fronts. One of these is the progress which can be or might be made in the Paris talks. An announcement of a fixed timetable for our withdrawal would completely remove any incentive for the enemy to negotiate an agreement. They would simply wait until our forces had withdrawn and then move in.

The other two factors on which we will base our withdrawal decisions are the level of enemy activity and the progress of the training programs of the South Vietnamese forces. And I am glad to be able to report tonight progress on both of these fronts has been greater than we anticipated when we started the program in June for withdrawal. As a result, our timetable for withdrawal is more optimistic now than when we made our first estimates in June. Now, this clearly demonstrates why it is not wise to be frozen in on a fixed timetable.

We must retain the flexibility to base each withdrawal decision on the situation as it is at the time rather than on estimates that are no longer valid.

Along with this optimistic estimate, I must in all candor leave one note of caution.

If the level of enemy activity significantly increases we might have to adjust our timetable accordingly. However, I want the record to be completely clear on one point. At the time of the bombing halt just a year ago, there was some confusion as to whether there was an understanding on the part of the enemy that if we stopped the bombing of North Vietnam they would stop the shelling of cities in South Vietnam.

I want to be sure that there is no misunderstanding on the part of the enemy with regard to our withdrawal program. We have noted the reduced level of infiltration, the reduction of our casualties, and are basing our withdrawal decisions partially on those factors.

If the level of infiltration or our casualties increase while we are trying to scale down the fighting, it will be the result of a conscious decision by the enemy. Hanoi could make no greater mistake than to assume that an increase in violence will be to its advantage. If I conclude that increased enemy action jeopardizes our remaining forces in Vietnam, I shall not hesitate to take strong and effective measures to deal with that situation.

This is not a threat. This is a statement of policy, which, as Commander in Chief of our Armed Forces, I am making in meeting my responsibility for the protection of American fighting men wherever they may be.

My fellow Americans, I am sure you can recognize from what I have said that we really only have two choices open to us if we want to end this war.

—I can order an immediate, precipitate withdrawal of all Americans from Vietnam without regard to the effects of that action.

—Or we can persist in our search for a just peace through a negotiated settlement if possible, or through continued implementation of our plan for Vietnamization if necessary a plan in which we will withdraw all our forces from Vietnam on a schedule in accordance with our program, as the South Vietnamese become strong enough to defend their own freedom. I have chosen this second course. It is not the easy way.

It is the right way. It is a plan which will end the war and serve the cause of peace not just in Vietnam but in the Pacific and in the world.

In speaking of the consequences of a precipitate withdrawal, I mentioned that our allies would lose confidence in America. Far more dangerous, we would lose confidence in ourselves. Oh, the immediate reaction would be a sense of relief that our men were coming home. But as we saw the consequences of what we had done, inevitable remorse and divisive recrimination would scar our spirit as a people.

We have faced other crises in our history and have become stronger by rejecting the easy way out and taking the right way in meeting our challenges. Our greatness as a nation has been our capacity to do what had to be done when we knew our course was right.

I recognize that some of my fellow citizens disagree with the plan for peace I have chosen. Honest and patriotic Americans have reached different conclusions as to how peace should be achieved.

In San Francisco a few weeks ago, I saw demonstrators carrying signs reading: "Lose in Vietnam, bring the boys home." Well, one of the strengths of our free society is that any American has a right to reach that conclusion and to advocate that point of view. But as President of the United States, I would be untrue to my oath of office if

I allowed the policy of this Nation to be dictated by the minority who hold that point of view and who try to impose it on the Nation by mounting demonstrations in the street.

For almost two hundred years, the policy of this Nation has been made under our Constitution by those leaders in the Congress and the White House elected by all of the people. If a vocal minority, however fervent its cause, prevails over reason and the will of the majority, this Nation has no future as a free society. And now I would like to address a word, if I may, to the young people of this Nation who are particularly concerned, and I understand why they are concerned, about this war. I respect your idealism. I share your concern for peace. I want peace as much as you do.

There are powerful personal reasons I want to end this war. This week I will have to sign eighty-three letters to mothers, fathers, wives, and loved ones of men who have given their lives for America in Vietnam. It is very little satisfaction to me that this is only one-third as many letters as I signed the first week in office. There is nothing I want more than to see the day come when I do not have to write any of those letters.

—I want to end the war to save the lives of those brave young men in Vietnam.

—But I want to end it in a way which will increase the chance that their younger brothers and their sons will not have to fight in some future Vietnam someplace in the world.

—And I want to end the war for another reason. I want to end it so that the energy and dedication of you, our young people, now too often directed into bitter hatred against those responsible for the war, can be turned to the great challenges of peace, a better life for all Americans, a better life for all people on this earth.

I have chosen a plan for peace. I believe it will succeed. If it does succeed, what the critics say now won't matter. If it does not succeed, anything I say then won't matter. I know it may not be fashionable to speak of patriotism or national destiny these days. But I feel it is appropriate to do so on this occasion. Two hundred years ago this Nation was weak and poor. But even then, America was the hope of millions in the world. Today we have become the strongest and richest nation in the world. And the wheel of destiny has turned so that any hope the world has for the survival of peace and freedom will be determined by whether the American people have the moral stamina and the courage to meet the challenge of free world leadership.

Let historians not record that when America was the most powerful nation in the world we passed on the other side of the road and allowed the last hopes for peace and freedom of millions of people to be suffocated by the forces of totalitarianism.

And so tonight to you, the great silent majority of my fellow Americans, I ask for your support. I pledged in my campaign for the Presidency to end the war in a way that we could win the peace. I have initiated a plan of action which will enable me to keep that pledge.

The more support I can have from the American people, the sooner that pledge can be redeemed; for the more divided we are at home, the less likely the enemy is to negotiate at Paris.

Let us be united for peace. Let us also be united against defeat. Because let us understand: North Vietnam cannot defeat or humiliate the United States. Only Americans can do that.

Fifty years ago, in this room and at this very desk, President Woodrow Wilson spoke words which caught the imagination of a war-weary world. He said: "This is the war to end war." His dream for peace after World War I was shattered on the hard realities of great power politics and Woodrow Wilson died a broken man.

Tonight I do not tell you that the war in Vietnam is the war to end wars. But I do say this: I have initiated a plan which will end this war in a way that will bring us closer to that great goal to which Woodrow Wilson and every American president in our history has been dedicated the goal of a just and lasting peace. As president I hold the responsibility for choosing the best path to that goal and then leading the Nation along it.

I pledge to you tonight that I shall meet this responsibility with all of the strength and wisdom I can command in accordance with your hopes, mindful of your concerns, sustained by your prayers.

Thank you and good night.

6

JIMMY CARTER, STATE OF THE UNION ADDRESS 1980[26]

January 23, 1980

This last few months has not been an easy time for any of us. As we meet tonight, it has never been more clear that the state of our Union depends on the state of the world. And tonight, as throughout our own generation, freedom and peace in the world depend on the state of our Union.

The 1980s have been born in turmoil, strife, and change. This is a time of challenge to our interests and our values and it's a time that tests our wisdom and our skills.

At this time in Iran, fifty Americans are still held captive, innocent victims of terrorism and anarchy. Also at this moment, massive Soviet troops are attempting to subjugate the fiercely independent and deeply religious people of Afghanistan. These two acts—one of international terrorism and one of military aggression—present a serious challenge to the United States of America and indeed to all the nations of the world. Together, we will meet these threats to peace.

---

[26] www.**jimmycarterlibrary.org**/documents/speeches/su80jec.phtml

I'm determined that the United States will remain the strongest of all nations, but our power will never be used to initiate a threat to the security of any nation or to the rights of any human being. We seek to be and to remain secure—a nation at peace in a stable world. But to be secure we must face the world as it is.

Three basic developments have helped to shape our challenges: the steady growth and increased projection of Soviet military power beyond its own borders; the overwhelming dependence of the Western democracies on oil supplies from the Middle East; and the press of social and religious and economic and political change in the many nations of the developing world, exemplified by the revolution in Iran.

Each of these factors is important in its own right. Each interacts with the others. All must be faced together, squarely and courageously. We will face these challenges, and we will meet them with the best that is in us. And we will not fail.

In response to the abhorrent act in Iran, our Nation has never been aroused and unified so greatly in peacetime. Our position is clear. The United States will not yield to blackmail.

We continue to pursue these specific goals: first, to protect the present and long-range interests of the United States; secondly, to preserve the lives of the American hostages and to secure, as quickly as possible, their safe release, if possible, to avoid bloodshed which might further endanger the lives of our fellow citizens; to enlist the help of other nations in condemning this act of violence, which is shocking and violates the moral and the legal standards of a civilized world; and also to convince and to persuade the Iranian leaders that the real danger to their nation lies in the north, in the Soviet Union and from the Soviet troops now in Afghanistan, and that the unwarranted Iranian quarrel with the United States hampers their response to this far greater danger to them.

If the American hostages are harmed, a severe price will be paid. We will never rest until every one of the American hostages are released.

But now we face a broader and more fundamental challenge in this region because of the recent military action of the Soviet Union.

Now, as during the last 3 1/2 decades, the relationship between our country, the United States of America, and the Soviet Union is the most critical factor in determining whether the world will live at peace or be engulfed in global conflict.

Since the end of the Second World War, America has led other nations in meeting the challenge of mounting Soviet power. This has not been a simple or a static relationship. Between us there has been cooperation, there has been competition, and at times there has been confrontation.

In the 1940s we took the lead in creating the Atlantic Alliance in response to the Soviet Union's suppression and then consolidation of its East European empire and the resulting threat of the Warsaw Pact to Western Europe.

In the 1950s we helped to contain further Soviet challenges in Korea and in the Middle East, and we rearmed to assure the continuation of that containment.

In the 1960s we met the Soviet challenges in Berlin, and we faced the Cuban missile crisis. And we sought to engage the Soviet Union in the important task of moving beyond the Cold War and away from confrontation.

And in the 1970s three American Presidents negotiated with the Soviet leaders in attempts to halt the growth of the nuclear arms race. We sought to establish rules of behavior that would reduce the risks of conflict, and we searched for areas of cooperation that could make our relations reciprocal and productive, not only for the sake of our two nations but for the security and peace of the entire world.

In all these actions, we have maintained two commitments: to be ready to meet any challenge by Soviet military power, and to develop ways to resolve disputes and to keep the peace.

Preventing nuclear war is the foremost responsibility of the two superpowers. That's why we've negotiated the strategic arms limitation treaties—SALT I and SALT II. Especially now, in a time of great tension, observing the mutual constraints imposed by the terms of these treaties will be in the best interest of both countries and will help to preserve world peace. I will consult very closely with the Congress on this matter as we strive to control nuclear weapons. That effort to control nuclear weapons will not be abandoned.

We superpowers also have the responsibility to exercise restraint in the use of our great military force. The integrity and the independence of weaker nations must not be threatened. They must know that in our presence they are secure.

But now the Soviet Union has taken a radical and an aggressive new step. It's using its great military power against a relatively defenseless nation. The implications of the Soviet invasion of Afghanistan could pose the most serious threat to the peace since the Second World War.

The vast majority of nations on Earth have condemned this latest Soviet attempt to extend its colonial domination of others and have demanded the immediate withdrawal of Soviet troops. The Moslem world is especially and justifiably outraged by this aggression against an Islamic people. No action of a world power has ever been so quickly and so overwhelmingly condemned. But verbal condemnation is not enough. The Soviet Union must pay a concrete price for their aggression.

While this invasion continues, we and the other nations of the world cannot conduct business as usual with the Soviet Union. That's why the United States has imposed stiff economic penalties on the Soviet Union. I will not issue any permits for Soviet ships to fish in the coastal waters of the United States. I've cut Soviet access to high-technology equipment and to agricultural products. I've limited other commerce with the Soviet Union, and I've asked our allies and friends to join with us in restraining their own trade with the Soviets and not to replace our own embargoed items. And I have notified the Olympic Committee that with Soviet invading forces in Afghanistan, neither the American people nor I will support sending an Olympic team to Moscow.

The Soviet Union is going to have to answer some basic questions: Will it help promote a more stable international environment in which its own legitimate, peaceful concerns can be pursued? Or will it continue to expand its military power far beyond its genuine security needs, and use that power for colonial conquest? The Soviet Union must realize that its decision to use military force in Afghanistan will be costly to every political and economic relationship it values.

The region which is now threatened by Soviet troops in Afghanistan is of great strategic importance: It contains more than two-thirds of the world's exportable oil. The Soviet effort to dominate Afghanistan has brought Soviet military forces to within three hundred miles of the Indian Ocean and close to the Straits of Hormuz, a waterway through which most of the world's oil must flow. The Soviet Union is now attempting to consolidate a strategic position, therefore, that poses a grave threat to the free movement of Middle East oil.

This situation demands careful thought, steady nerves, and resolute action, not only for this year but for many years to come. It demands collective efforts to meet this new threat to security in the Persian Gulf and in Southwest Asia. It demands the participation of all those who rely on oil from the Middle East and who are concerned with global peace and stability. And it demands consultation and close cooperation with countries in the area which might be threatened.

Meeting this challenge will take national will, diplomatic and political wisdom, economic sacrifice, and, of course, military capability. We must call on the best that is in us to preserve the security of this crucial region.

Let our position be absolutely clear: An attempt by any outside force to gain control of the Persian Gulf region will be regarded as an assault on the vital interests of the United States of America, and such an assault will be repelled by any means necessary, including military force.

During the past three years, you have joined with me to improve our own security and the prospects for peace, not only in the vital oil-producing area of the Persian Gulf region but around the world. We've increased annually our real commitment for defense, and we will sustain this increase of effort throughout the Five Year Defense Program. It's imperative that Congress approve this strong defense budget for 1981, encompassing a 5 percent real growth in authorizations, without any reduction.

We are also improving our capability to deploy U.S. military forces rapidly to distant areas. We've helped to strengthen NATO and our other alliances, and recently we and other NATO members have decided to develop and to deploy modernized, intermediate-range nuclear forces to meet an unwarranted and increased threat from the nuclear weapons of the Soviet Union.

We are working with our allies to prevent conflict in the Middle East. The peace treaty between Egypt and Israel is a notable achievement which represents a strategic asset for America and which also enhances prospects for regional and world peace. We are now engaged in further negotiations to provide full autonomy for the people of the West Bank and Gaza, to resolve the Palestinian issue in all its aspects, and to preserve the peace and security of Israel. Let no one doubt our commitment to the security of Israel. In a few days we will observe an historic event when Israel makes another major withdrawal from the Sinai and when Ambassadors will be exchanged between Israel and Egypt.

We've also expanded our own sphere of friendship. Our deep commitment to human rights and to meeting human needs has improved our relationship with much of the Third World. Our decision to normalize relations with the People's Republic of China will help to preserve peace and stability in Asia and in the Western Pacific.

We've increased and strengthened our naval presence in the Indian Ocean, and we are now making arrangements for key naval and air facilities to be used by our forces in the region of northeast Africa and the Persian Gulf.

We've reconfirmed our 1959 agreement to help Pakistan preserve its independence and its integrity. The United States will take action consistent with our own laws to assist Pakistan in resisting any outside aggression. And I'm asking the Congress specifically to reaffirm this agreement. I'm also working, along with the leaders of other nations, to provide additional military and economic aid for Pakistan. That request will come to you in just a few days.

In the weeks ahead, we will further strengthen political and military ties with other nations in the region. We believe that there are no irreconcilable differences between us and any Islamic nation. We respect the faith of Islam, and we are ready to cooperate with all Moslem countries.

Finally, we are prepared to work with other countries in the region to share a cooperative security framework that respects differing values and political beliefs, yet which enhances the independence, security, and prosperity of all.

All these efforts combined emphasize our dedication to defend and preserve the vital interests of the region and of the nation which we represent and those of our allies—in Europe and the Pacific, and also in the parts of the world which have such great strategic importance to us, stretching especially through the Middle East and Southwest Asia. With your help, I will pursue these efforts with vigor and with determination. You and I will act as necessary to protect and to preserve our Nation's security.

The men and women of America's Armed Forces are on duty tonight in many parts of the world. I'm proud of the job they are doing, and I know you share that pride. I believe that our volunteer forces are adequate for current defense needs, and I hope that it will not become necessary to impose a draft. However, we must be prepared for that possibility. For this reason, I have determined that the Selective Service System must now be revitalized. I will send legislation and budget proposals to the Congress next month so that we can begin registration and then meet future mobilization needs rapidly if they arise.

We also need clear and quick passage of a new charter to define the legal authority and accountability of our intelligence agencies. We will guarantee that abuses do not recur, but we must tighten our controls on sensitive intelligence information, and we need to remove unwarranted restraints on America's ability to collect intelligence.

The decade ahead will be a time of rapid change, as nations everywhere seek to deal with new problems and age-old tensions. But America need have no fear. We can thrive in a world of change if we remain true to our values and actively engaged in promoting world peace. We will continue to work as we have for peace in the Middle East and southern Africa. We will continue to build our ties with developing nations, respecting and helping to strengthen their national independence which they have struggled so hard to achieve. And we will continue to support the growth of democracy and the protection of human rights.

In repressive regimes, popular frustrations often have no outlet except through violence. But when peoples and their governments can approach their problems together through open, democratic methods, the basis for stability and peace is far more solid and far more enduring. That is why our support for human rights in other countries is in our own national interest as well as part of our own national character.

Peace—a peace that preserves freedom-remains America's first goal. In the coming years, as a mighty nation we will continue to pursue peace. But to be strong abroad we must be strong at home. And in order to be strong, we must continue to face up to the difficult issues that confront us as a nation today.

The crises in Iran and Afghanistan have dramatized a very important lesson: Our excessive dependence on foreign oil is a clear and present danger to our Nation's security. The need has never been more urgent. At long last, we must have a clear, comprehensive energy policy for the United States.

As you well know, I have been working with the Congress in a concentrated and persistent way over the past three years to meet this need. We have made progress together. But Congress must act promptly now to complete final action on this vital energy legislation. Our Nation will then have a major conservation effort, important initiatives to develop solar power, realistic pricing based on the true value of oil, strong incentives for the production of coal and other fossil fuels in the United States, and our Nation's most massive peacetime investment in the development of synthetic fuels.

The American people are making progress in energy conservation. Last year we reduced overall petroleum consumption by 8 percent and gasoline consumption by 5 percent below what it was the year before. Now we must do more.

After consultation with the Governors, we will set gasoline conservation goals for each of the fifty States, and I will make them mandatory if these goals are not met.

I've established an import ceiling for 1980 of 8.2 million barrels a day—well below the level of foreign oil purchases in 1977. I expect our imports to be much lower than this, but the ceiling will be enforced by an oil import fee if necessary. I'm prepared to lower these imports still further if the other oil-consuming countries will join us in a fair and mutual reduction. If we have a serious shortage, I will not hesitate to impose mandatory gasoline rationing immediately.

The single biggest factor in the inflation rate last year, the increase in the inflation rate last year, was from one cause: the skyrocketing prices of OPEC oil. We must take whatever actions are necessary to reduce our dependence on foreign oil—and at the same time reduce inflation.

As individuals and as families, few of us can produce energy by ourselves. But all of us can conserve energy—every one of us, every day of our lives. Tonight I call on you—in fact, all the people of America—to help our Nation. Conserve energy. Eliminate waste. Make 1980 indeed a year of energy conservation.

Of course, we must take other actions to strengthen our Nation's economy.

First, we will continue to reduce the deficit and then to balance the Federal budget.

Second, as we continue to work with business to hold down prices, we'll build also on the historic national accord with organized labor to restrain pay increases in a fair fight against inflation.

Third, we will continue our successful efforts to cut paperwork and to dismantle unnecessary Government regulation.

Fourth, we will continue our progress in providing jobs for America, concentrating on a major new program to provide training and work for our young people, especially minority youth. It has been said that "a mind is a terrible thing to waste." We will give our young people new hope for jobs and a better life in the 1980s.

And fifth, we must use the decade of the 1980s to attack the basic structural weaknesses and problems in our economy through measures to increase productivity, savings, and investment.

With these energy and economic policies, we will make America even stronger at home in this decade—just as our foreign and defense policies will make us stronger and safer throughout the world. We will never abandon our struggle for a just and a decent society here at home. That's the heart of America—and it's the source of our ability to inspire other people to defend their own rights abroad.

Our material resources, great as they are, are limited. Our problems are too complex for simple slogans or for quick solutions. We cannot solve them without effort and sacrifice. Walter Lippmann once reminded us, "You took the good things for granted. Now you must earn them again. For every right that you cherish, you have a duty which you must fulfill. For every good which you wish to preserve, you will have to sacrifice your comfort and your ease. There is nothing for nothing any longer."

Our challenges are formidable. But there's a new spirit of unity and resolve in our country. We move into the 1980s with confidence and hope and a bright vision of the America we want: an America strong and free, an America at peace, an America with equal rights for all citizens—and for women, guaranteed in the United States Constitution—an America with jobs and good health and good education for every citizen, an America with a clean and bountiful life in our cities and on our farms, an America that helps to feed the world, an America secure in filling its own energy needs, an America of justice, tolerance, and compassion. For this vision to come true, we must sacrifice, but this national commitment will be an exciting enterprise that will unify our people.

Together as one people, let us work to build our strength at home, and together as one indivisible union, let us seek peace and security throughout the world.

Together let us make of this time of challenge and danger a decade of national resolve and of brave achievement.

Thank you very much.

7A
RONALD REAGAN

Excerpt from the Inaugural Address January 20, 1981[27]

Well, I believe we, the Americans of today, are ready to act worthy of ourselves, ready to do what must be done to ensure happiness and liberty for ourselves, our children and our children's children.

And as we renew ourselves here in our own land, we will be seen as having greater strength throughout the world. We will again be the exemplar of freedom and a beacon of hope for those who do not now have freedom.

To those neighbors and allies who share our freedom, we will strengthen our historic ties and assure them of our support and firm commitment. We will match loyalty with loyalty. We will strive for mutually beneficial relations. We will not use our friendship to impose on their sovereignty, for our own sovereignty is not for sale.

As for the enemies of freedom, those who are potential adversaries, they will be reminded that peace is the highest aspiration of the American people. We will negotiate for it, sacrifice for it; we will not surrender for it—now or ever.

---

[27] www.yale.edu/lawweb/avalon/presiden/inaug/reagan1.htm

Our forbearance should never be misunderstood. Our reluctance for conflict should not be misjudged as a failure of will. When action is required to preserve our national security, we will act. We will maintain sufficient strength to prevail if need be, knowing that if we do so we have the best chance of never having to use that strength.

Above all, we must realize that no arsenal, or no weapon in the arsenals of the world, is so formidable as the will and moral courage of free men and women. It is a weapon our adversaries in today's world do not have. It is a weapon that we as Americans do have. Let that be understood by those who practice terrorism and prey upon their neighbors.

7B
RONALD REAGAN

Address to the Nation, February 6, 1985[28]

Mr. Speaker, Mr. President, distinguished Members of the Congress, honored guests, and fellow citizens:

I come before you to report on the state of our Union, and I'm pleased to report that after four years of united effort, the American people have brought forth a nation renewed, stronger, freer, and more secure than before.

Four years ago we began to change, forever I hope, our assumptions about government and its place in our lives. Out of that change has come great and robust growth—in our confidence, our economy, and our role in the world.

Tonight America is stronger because of the values that we hold dear. We believe faith and freedom must be our guiding stars, for they show us truth, they make us brave, give us hope, and leave us wiser than we were. Our progress began not in Washington, DC, but in the hearts of our families, communities, workplaces, and voluntary groups which, together, are unleashing the invincible spirit of one great nation under God.

---

[28] www.yale.edu/lawweb/avalon/presiden/inaug/reagan2.htm

Four years ago we said we would invigorate our economy by giving people greater freedom and incentives to take risks and letting them keep more of what they earned. We did what we promised, and a great industrial giant is reborn.

Tonight we can take pride in twenty-five straight months of economic growth, the strongest in thirty-four years; a three-year inflation average of 3.9 percent, the lowest in seventeen years; and 7.3 million new jobs in two years, with more of our citizens working than ever before.

New freedom in our lives has planted the rich seeds for future success:

For an America of wisdom that honors the family, knowing that if (as) the family goes, so goes our civilization;

For an America of vision that sees tomorrow's dreams in the learning and hard work we do today;

For an America of courage whose service men and women, even as we meet, proudly stand watch on the frontiers of freedom;

For an America of compassion that opens its heart to those who cry out for help.

We have begun well. But it's only a beginning. We're not here to congratulate ourselves on what we have done but to challenge ourselves to finish what has not yet been done.

We're here to speak for millions in our inner cities who long for real jobs, safe neighborhoods, and schools that truly teach. We're here to speak for the American farmer, the entrepreneur, and every worker in industries fighting to modernize and compete. And, yes, we're here to stand, and proudly so, for all who struggle to break free from totalitarianism, for all who know in their hearts that freedom is the one true path to peace and human happiness.

Proverbs tell us, without a vision the people perish. When asked what great principle holds our Union together, Abraham Lincoln said: "Something in (the) Declaration giving liberty, not alone to the people of this country, but hope to the world for all future time."

We honor the giants of our history not by going back but forward to the dreams their vision foresaw. My fellow citizens, this nation is poised for greatness. The time has come to proceed toward a great new challenge—a second American Revolution of hope and opportunity; a revolution carrying us to new heights of progress by pushing back frontiers of knowledge and space; a revolution of spirit that taps the soul of America, enabling us to summon greater strength than we've ever known; and a revolution that carries beyond our shores the golden promise of human freedom in a world of peace.

Let us begin by challenging our conventional wisdom. There are no constraints on the human mind, no walls around the human spirit, no barriers to our progress except those we ourselves erect. Already, pushing down tax rates has freed our economy to vault forward to record growth.

In Europe, they're calling it "the American Miracle." Day by day, we're shattering accepted notions of what is possible. When I was growing up, we failed to see how a new thing called radio would transform our marketplace. Well, today, many have not yet seen how advances in technology are transforming our lives.

In the late 1950s workers at the AT&T semiconductor plant in Pennsylvania produced five transistors a day for $7.50 apiece. They now produce over a million for less than a penny apiece.

New laser techniques could revolutionize heart bypass surgery, cut diagnosis time for viruses linked to cancer from weeks to minutes, reduce hospital costs dramatically, and hold out new promise for saving human lives.

Our automobile industry has overhauled assembly lines, increased worker productivity, and is competitive once again.

We stand on the threshold of a great ability to produce more, do more, be more. Our economy is not getting older and weaker; it's getting younger and stronger. It doesn't need rest and supervision; it needs new challenge, greater freedom. And that word "freedom" is the key to the second American revolution that we need to bring about.

Let us move together with an historic reform of tax simplification for fairness and growth. Last year I asked Treasury Secretary-then-Regan to develop a plan to simplify the tax code, so all taxpayers would be treated more fairly and personal tax rates could come further down.

We have cut tax rates by almost twenty-five percent, yet the tax system remains unfair and limits our potential for growth. Exclusions and exemptions cause similar incomes to be taxed at different levels. Low-income families face steep tax barriers that make hard lives even harder. The Treasury Department has produced an excellent reform plan, whose principles will guide the final proposal that we will ask you to enact.

One thing that tax reform will not be is a tax increase in disguise. We will not jeopardize the mortgage interest deduction that families need. We will reduce personal tax rates as low as possible by removing many tax preferences. We will propose a top rate of no more than 35 percent, and possibly lower. And we will propose reducing corporate rates, while maintaining incentives for capital formation.

To encourage opportunity and jobs rather than dependency and welfare, we will propose that individuals living at or near the poverty line be totally exempt from Federal income tax. To restore fairness to families, we will propose increasing significantly the personal exemption.

And tonight, I am instructing Treasury Secretary James Baker—I have to get used to saying that—to begin working with congressional authors and committees for bipartisan legislation conforming to these principles. We will call upon the American people for support and upon every man and woman in this Chamber. Together, we can pass, this year, a tax bill for fairness, simplicity, and growth, making this economy the engine of our dreams and America the investment capital of the world. So let us begin.

Tax simplification will be a giant step toward unleashing the tremendous pent-up power of our economy. But a second American revolution must carry the promise of opportunity for all. It is time to liberate the spirit of enterprise in the most distressed areas of our country.

This government will meet its responsibility to help those in need. But policies that increase dependency, break up families, and destroy self-respect are not progressive; they're reactionary. Despite our strides in civil rights, blacks, Hispanics, and all minorities will not have full and equal power until they have full economic power.

We have repeatedly sought passage of enterprise zones to help those in the abandoned corners of our land find jobs, learn skills, and build better lives. This legislation is supported by a majority of you.

Mr. Speaker, I know we agree that there must be no forgotten Americans. Let us place new dreams in a million hearts and create a new generation of entrepreneurs by passing enterprise zones this year. And, Tip, you could make that a birthday present.

Nor must we lose the chance to pass our youth employment opportunity wage proposal. We can help teenagers, who have the highest unemployment rate, find summer jobs, so they can know the pride of work and have confidence in their futures.

We'll continue to support the Job Training Partnership Act, which has a nearly two-thirds job placement rate. Credits in education and health care vouchers will help working families shop for services that they need.

Our administration is already encouraging certain low-income public housing residents to own and manage their own dwellings. It's time that all public housing residents have that opportunity of ownership.

The Federal Government can help create a new atmosphere of freedom. But States and localities, many of which enjoy surpluses from the recovery, must not permit their tax and regulatory policies to stand as barriers to growth.

Let us resolve that we will stop spreading dependency and start spreading opportunity; that we will stop spreading bondage and start spreading freedom.

There are some who say that growth initiatives must await final action on deficit reductions. Well, the best way to reduce deficits is through economic growth. More businesses will be started, more investments made, more jobs created, and more people will be on payrolls paying taxes. The best way to reduce government spending is to reduce the need for spending by increasing prosperity. Each added percentage point per year of real GNP growth will lead to cumulative reduction in deficits of nearly $200 billion over five years.

To move steadily toward a balanced budget, we must also lighten government's claim on our total economy. We will not do this by raising taxes. We must make sure that our economy grows faster than the growth in spending by the Federal Government. In our fiscal year 1986 budget, overall government program spending will be frozen at the current level. It must not be one dime higher than fiscal year 1985, and three points are key.

First, the social safety net for the elderly, the needy, the disabled, and unemployed will be left intact. Growth of our major health care programs, Medicare and Medicaid, will be slowed, but protections for the elderly and needy will be preserved.

Second, we must not relax our efforts to restore military strength just as we near our goal of a fully equipped, trained, and ready professional corps. National security is government's first responsibility; so in past years defense spending took about half the Federal budget. Today it takes less than a third. We've already reduced our planned defense expenditures by nearly a hundred billion dollars over the past four years and reduced projected spending again this year.

You know, we only have a military-industrial complex until a time of danger, and then it becomes the arsenal of democracy. Spending for defense is investing in things that are priceless—peace and freedom.

Third, we must reduce or eliminate costly government subsidies. For example, deregulation of the airline industry has led to cheaper airfares, but on Amtrak taxpayers pay about $35 per passenger every time an Amtrak train leaves the station, It's time we ended this huge Federal subsidy.

Our farm program costs have quadrupled in recent years. Yet I know from visiting farmers, many in great financial distress, that we need an orderly transition to a market-oriented farm economy. We can help farmers best not by expanding Federal payments but by making fundamental reforms, keeping interest rates heading down, and knocking down foreign trade barriers to American farm exports.

We're moving ahead with Grace commission reforms to eliminate waste and improve government's management practices. In the long run, we must protect the taxpayers from government. And I ask again that you pass, as thirty-two States have now called for, an amendment mandating the Federal Government spend no more than it takes in. And I ask for the authority, used responsibly by forty-three governors, to veto individual items in appropriation bills. Senator Mattingly has introduced a bill permitting a two-year trial run of the line-item veto. I hope you'll pass and send that legislation to my desk.

Nearly fifty years of government living beyond its means has brought us to a time of reckoning. Ours is but a moment in history. But one moment of courage, idealism, and bipartisan unity can change American history forever.

Sound monetary policy is key to long-running economic strength and stability. We will continue to cooperate with the Federal Reserve Board, seeking a steady policy that ensures price stability without keeping interest rates artificially high or needlessly holding down growth.

Reducing unneeded red tape and regulations, and deregulating the energy, transportation, and financial industries have unleashed new competition, giving consumers more choices, better services, and lower prices. In just one set of grant programs we have reduced 905 pages of regulations to thirty-one. We seek to fully deregulate natural gas to bring on new supplies and bring us closer to energy independence. Consistent with safety standards, we will continue removing restraints on the bus and railroad industries, we will soon end up legislation—or send up legislation, I should say—to return Conrail to the private sector where it belongs, and we will support further deregulation of the trucking industry.

Every dollar the Federal Government does not take from us, every decision it does not make for us will make our economy stronger, our lives more abundant, our future more free.

Our second American revolution will push on to new possibilities not only on Earth but in the next frontier of space. Despite budget restraints, we will seek record funding for research and development.

We've seen the success of the space shuttle. Now we're going to develop a permanently manned space station and new opportunities for free enterprise, because in the next decade Americans and our friends around the world will be living and working together in space.

In the zero gravity of space, we could manufacture in thirty days lifesaving medicines it would take thirty years to make on Earth. We can make crystals of exceptional purity to produce super computers, creating jobs, technologies, and medical breakthroughs beyond anything we ever dreamed possible.

As we do all this, we'll continue to protect our natural resources. We will seek reauthorization and expanded funding for the Superfund program to continue cleaning up hazardous waste sites which threaten human health and the environment.

Now, there's another great heritage to speak of this evening. Of all the changes that have swept America the past four years, none brings greater promise than our rediscovery of the values of faith, freedom, family, work, and neighborhood.

We see signs of renewal in increased attendance in places of worship; renewed optimism and faith in our future; love of country rediscovered by our young, who are leading the way. We've rediscovered that work is good in and of itself, that it ennobles us to create and contribute no matter how seemingly humble our jobs. We've seen a powerful new current from an old and honorable tradition-- American generosity.

From thousands answering Peace Corps appeals to help boost food production in Africa, to millions volunteering time, corporations adopting schools, and communities pulling together to help the neediest among us at home, we have refound our values. Private sector initiatives are crucial to our future.

I thank the Congress for passing equal access legislation giving religious groups the same right to use classrooms after school that other groups enjoy. But no citizen need tremble, nor the world shudder, if a child stands in a classroom and breathes a prayer. We ask you again, give children back a right they had for a century and a half or more in this country.

The question of abortion grips our nation. Abortion is either the taking of a human life or it isn't. And if it is—and medical technology is increasingly showing it is—it must be stopped. It is a terrible irony that while some turn to abortion, so many others who cannot become parents cry out for children to adopt. We have room for these children. We can fill the cradles of those who want a child to love. And tonight I ask you in the Congress to move this year on legislation to protect the unborn.

In the area of education, we're returning to excellence, and again, the heroes are our people, not government. We're stressing basics of discipline, rigorous testing, and homework, while helping children become computer-smart as well. For twenty years scholastic aptitude test scores of our high school students went down, but now they have gone up two of the last three years. We must go forward in our commitment to the new basics, giving parents greater authority and making sure good teachers are rewarded for hard work and achievement through merit pay.

Of all the changes in the past twenty years, none has more threatened our sense of national well-being than the explosion of violent crime. One does not have to be attacked to be a victim. The woman who must run to her car after shopping at night is a victim. The couple draping their door with locks and chains are victims; as is the tired, decent cleaning woman who can't ride a subway home without being afraid.

We do not seek to violate the rights of defendants. But shouldn't we feel more compassion for the victims of crime than for those who commit crime? For the first time in twenty years, the crime index has fallen two years in a row. We've convicted over 7,400 drug offenders and put them, as well as leaders of organized crime, behind bars in record numbers.

But we must do more. I urge the House to follow the Senate and enact proposals permitting use of all reliable evidence that police officers acquire in good faith. These proposals would also reform the habeas corpus laws and allow, in keeping with the will of the overwhelming majority of Americans, the use of the death penalty where necessary.

There can be no economic revival in ghettos when the most violent among us are allowed to roam free. It's time we restored domestic tranquility. And we mean to do just that.

Just as we're positioned as never before to secure justice in our economy, we're poised as never before to create a safer, freer, more peaceful world. Our alliances are stronger than ever. Our economy is stronger than ever. We have resumed our historic role as a leader of the free world. And all of these together are a great force for peace.

Since 1981 we've been committed to seeking fair and verifiable arms agreements that would lower the risk of war and reduce the size of nuclear arsenals. Now our determination to maintain a strong defense has influenced the Soviet Union to return to the bargaining table. Our negotiators must be able to go to that table with the united support of the American people. All of us have no greater dream than to see the day when nuclear weapons are banned from this Earth forever.

Each Member of the Congress has a role to play in modernizing our defenses, thus supporting our chances for a meaningful arms agreement. Your vote this spring on the Peacekeeper missile will be a critical test of our resolve to maintain the strength we need and move toward mutual and verifiable arms reductions.

For the past twenty years we've believed that no war will be launched as long as each side knows it can retaliate with a deadly counterstrike. Well, I believe there's a better way of eliminating the threat of nuclear war. It is a Strategic Defense Initiative aimed ultimately at finding a nonnuclear defense against ballistic missiles. It's the most hopeful possibility of the nuclear age. But it's not very well understood.

Some say it will bring war to the heavens, but its purpose is to deter war in the heavens and on Earth. Now, some say the research would be expensive. Perhaps, but it could save millions of lives, indeed humanity itself. And some say if we build such a system, the Soviets will build a defense system of their own. Well, they already have strategic defenses that surpass ours; a civil defense system, where we have almost none; and a research program covering roughly the same areas of technology that we're now exploring. And finally some say the research will take a long time. Well, the answer to that is: Let's get started.

Harry Truman once said that, ultimately, our security and the world's hopes for peace and human progress "lie not in measures of defense or in the control of weapons, but in the growth and expansion of freedom and self-government."

And tonight, we declare anew to our fellow citizens of the world: Freedom is not the sole prerogative of a chosen few; it is the universal right of all God's children. Look to where peace and prosperity flourish today. It is in homes that freedom built. Victories against poverty are greatest and peace most secure where people live by laws that ensure free press, free speech, and freedom to worship, vote, and create wealth.

Our mission is to nourish and defend freedom and democracy, and to communicate these ideals everywhere we can. America's economic success is freedom's success; it can be repeated a hundred times in a hundred different nations. Many countries in East Asia and the Pacific have few resources other than the enterprise of their own people. But through low tax rates and free markets they've soared ahead of centralized economies. And now China is opening up its economy to meet its needs.

We need a stronger and simpler approach to the process of making and implementing trade policy, and we'll be studying potential changes in that process in the next few weeks. We've seen the benefits of free trade and lived through the disasters of protectionism. Tonight I ask all our trading partners, developed and developing alike, to join us in a new round of trade negotiations to expand trade and competition and strengthen the global economy--and to begin it in this next year.

There are more than three billion human beings living in Third World countries with an average per capita income of $650 a year. Many are victims of dictatorships that impoverished them with taxation and corruption. Let us ask our allies to join us in a practical program of trade and assistance that fosters economic development through personal incentives to help these people climb from poverty on their own.

We cannot play innocents abroad in a world that's not innocent; nor can we be passive when freedom is under siege. Without resources, diplomacy cannot succeed. Our security assistance programs help friendly governments defend themselves and give them confidence to work for peace. And I hope that you in the Congress will understand that, dollar for dollar, security assistance contributes as much to global security as our own defense budget.

We must stand by all our democratic allies. And we must not break faith with those who are risking their lives—on every continent, from Afghanistan to Nicaragua—to defy Soviet-supported aggression and secure rights which have been ours from birth.

The Sandinista dictatorship of Nicaragua, with full Cuban-Soviet bloc support, not only persecutes its people, the church, and denies a free press, but arms and provides bases for Communist terrorists attacking neighboring states. Support for freedom fighters is self-defense and totally consistent with the OAS and U.N. Charters. It is essential that the Congress continue all facets of our assistance to Central America. I want to work with you to support the democratic forces whose struggle is tied to our own security.

And tonight, I've spoken of great plans and great dreams. They're dreams we can make come true. Two hundred years of American history should have taught us that nothing is impossible.

Ten years ago a young girl left Vietnam with her family, part of the exodus that followed the fall of Saigon. They came to the United States with no possessions and not knowing a word of English. Ten years ago—the young girl studied hard, learned English, and finished high school in the top of her class. And this May, May 22nd to be exact, is a big date on her calendar. Just ten years from the time she left Vietnam, she will graduate from the United States Military Academy at West Point. I thought you might like to meet an American hero named Jean Nguyen.

Now, there's someone else here tonight, born seventy-nine years ago. She lives in the inner city, where she cares for infants born of mothers who are heroin addicts. The children, born in withdrawal, are sometimes even dropped on her doorstep. She helps them with love. Go to her house some night, and maybe you'll see her silhouette against the window as she walks the floor talking softly, soothing a child in her arms—Mother Hale of Harlem, and she, too, is an American hero.

Jean, Mother Hale, your lives tell us that the oldest American saying is new again: Anything is possible in America if we have the faith, the will, and the heart. History is asking us once again to be a force for good in the world. Let us begin in unity, with justice, and love.

Thank you, and God bless you.

Note: The president spoke at 9:05 PM in the House Chamber of the Capitol. He was introduced by Thomas P. O'Neill, Jr., Speaker of the House of Representatives. The address was broadcast live on nationwide radio and television.

8

CASPER W. WEINBERGER "THE USES OF MILITARY POWER"

November 28, 1984

Thank you for inviting me to be here today with the members of the National Press Club, a group most important to our national security. I say that because a major point I intend to make in my remarks today is that the single most critical element of a successful democracy is a strong consensus of support and agreement for our basic purposes.

Policies formed without a clear understanding of what we hope to achieve will never work. And you help to build that understanding among our citizens.

Of all the many policies our citizens deserve and need to understand, none is so important as those related to our topic today the uses of military power. Deterrence will work only if the Soviets understand our firm commitment to keeping the peace ... and only from a well-informed public can we expect to have that national will and commitment.

---

[29] www.**pbs.org**/wgbh/pages/frontline/shows/**military**/force/**weinberger**.htm

So today, I want to discuss with you perhaps the most important question concerning keeping the peace. Under what circumstances, and by what means, does a great democracy such as ours reach the painful decision that the use of military force is necessary to protect our interests or to carry out our national policy?

National power has many components, some tangible, like economic wealth, technical pre-eminence. Other components are intangible such as moral force, or strong national will. Military forces, when they are strong and ready and modern, are a credible and tangible addition to a nation's power. When both the intangible national will and those forces are forged into one instrument, national power becomes effective.

In today's world, the line between peace and war is less clearly drawn than at any time in our history. When George Washington, in his farewell address, warned us, as a new democracy, to avoid foreign entanglements, Europe then lay two–three months by sea over the horizon. The United States was protected by the width of the oceans. Now in this nuclear age, we measure time in minutes rather than months.

Aware of the consequences of any misstep, yet convinced of the precious worth of the freedom we enjoy, we seek to avoid conflict, while maintaining strong defenses. Our policy has always been to work hard for peace, but to be prepared if war comes. Yet, so blurred have the lines become between open conflict and half-hidden hostile acts that we cannot confidently predict where, or when, or how, or from what direction aggression may arrive. We must be prepared, at any moment, to meet threats ranging in intensity from isolated terrorist acts, to guerrilla action, to full-scale military confrontation.

Alexander Hamilton, writing in the Federalist Papers, said that it is impossible to foresee or define the extent and variety of national exigencies, or the correspondent extent and variety of the means, which may be necessary to satisfy them. If it was true then, how much more true it is today, when we must remain ready to consider the means to meet such serious indirect challenges to the peace as proxy wars and individual terrorist action. And how much more important is it now, considering the consequences of failing to deter conflict at the lowest level possible. While the use of military force to defend territory has never been questioned when a democracy has been attacked and its very survival threatened, most democracies have rejected the unilateral aggressive use of force to invade, conquer or subjugate other nations. The extent to which the use of force is acceptable remains unresolved for the host of other situations which fall between these extremes of defensive and aggressive use of force.

We find ourselves, then, face to face with a modern paradox: The most likely challenge to the peace the gray area conflicts are precisely the most difficult challenges to which a democracy must respond. Yet, while the source and nature of today's challenges are uncertain, our response must be clear and understandable. Unless we are certain that force is essential, we run the risk of inadequate national will to apply the resources needed.

Because we face a spectrum of threats from covert aggression, terrorism, and subversion, to overt intimidation, to use of brute force choosing the appropriate level of our response is difficult. Flexible response does not mean just any response is appropriate. But once a decision to employ some degree of force has been made, and the purpose clarified, our government must have the clear mandate to carry out, and continue to carry out, that decision until the purpose has been achieved. That, too, has been difficult to accomplish.

The issue of which branch of government has authority to define that mandate and make decisions on using force is now being strongly contended. Beginning in the 1970s Congress demanded, and assumed, a far more active role in the making of foreign policy and in the decision-making process for the employment of military forces abroad than had been thought appropriate and practical before. As a result, the centrality of decision-making authority in the Executive branch has been compromised by the Legislative branch to an extent that actively interferes with that process. At the same time, there has not been a corresponding acceptance of responsibility by Congress for the outcome of decisions concerning the employment of military forces.

Yet the outcome of decisions on whether and when and to what degree to use combat forces abroad has never been more important than it is today. While we do not seek to deter or settle all the world's conflicts, we must recognize that, as a major power, our responsibilities and interests are now of such scope that there are few troubled areas we can afford to ignore. So we must be prepared to deal with a range of possibilities, a spectrum of crises, from local insurgency to global conflict. We prefer, of course, to limit any conflict in its early stages, to contain and control it but to do that our military forces must be deployed in a timely manner, and be fully supported and prepared before they are engaged, because many of those difficult decisions must be made extremely quickly.

Some on the national scene think they can always avoid making tough decisions. Some reject entirely the question of whether any force can ever be used abroad. They want to avoid grappling with a complex issue because, despite clever rhetoric disguising their purpose, these people are in fact advocating a return to post-World War I isolationism.

While they may maintain in principle that military force has a role in foreign policy, they are never willing to name the circumstance or the place where it would apply.

On the other side, some theorists argue that military force can be brought to bear in any crisis. Some of these proponents of force are eager to advocate its use even in limited amounts simply because they believe that if there are American forces of any size present they will somehow solve the problem.

Neither of these two extremes offers us any lasting or satisfactory solutions. The first undue reserve would lead us ultimately to withdraw from international events that require free nations to defend their interests from the aggressive use of force. We would be abdicating our responsibilities as the leader of the free world responsibilities more or less thrust upon us in the aftermath of World War II war incidentally that isolationism did nothing to deter. These are responsibilities we must fulfill unless we desire the Soviet Union to keep expanding its influence unchecked throughout the world. In an international system based on mutual interdependence among nations, and alliances between friends, stark isolationism quickly would lead to a far more dangerous situation for the United States: we would be without allies and faced by many hostile or indifferent nations.

The second alternative employing our forces almost indiscriminately and as a regular and customary part of our diplomatic efforts would surely plunge us headlong into the sort of domestic turmoil we experienced during the Vietnam war, without accomplishing the goal for which we committed our forces. Such policies might very well tear at the fabric of our society, endangering the single most critical element of a successful democracy: a strong consensus of support and agreement for our basic purposes.

Policies formed without a clear understanding of what we hope to achieve would also earn us the scorn of our troops, who would have an understandable opposition to being used in every sense of the word casually and without intent to support them fully.

Ultimately this course would reduce their morale and their effectiveness for engagements we must win. And if the military were to distrust its civilian leadership, recruitment would fall off and I fear an end to the all-volunteer system would be upon us, requiring a return to a draft, sowing the seeds of riot and discontent that so wracked the country in the sixties.

We have now restored high morale and pride in the uniform throughout the services. The all-volunteer system is working spectacularly well. Are we willing to forfeit what we have fought so hard to regain?

In maintaining our progress in strengthening America's military deterrent, we face difficult challenges. For we have entered an era where the dividing lines between peace and war are less clearly drawn, the identity of the foe is much less clear. In World Wars I and II, we not only knew who our enemies were, but we shared a clear sense of why the principles espoused by our enemies were unworthy.

Since these two wars threatened our very survival as a free nation and the survival of our allies, they were total wars, involving every aspect of our society. All our means of production, all our resources were devoted to winning. Our policies had the unqualified support of the great majority of our people. Indeed, World Wars I and II ended with the unconditional surrender of our enemies....The only acceptable ending when the alternative was the loss of our freedom.

But in the aftermath of the Second World War, we encountered a more subtle form of warfare in which, more often than not, the face of the enemy was masked. Territorial expansionism could be carried out indirectly by proxy powers, using surrogate forces aided and advised from afar. Some conflicts occurred under the name of "national liberation," but far more frequently ideology or religion provided the spark to the tinder.

Our adversaries can also take advantage of our open society, and our freedom of speech and opinion to use alarming rhetoric and disinformation to divide and disrupt our unity of purpose. While they would never dare to allow such freedoms to their own people, they are quick to exploit ours by conducting simultaneous military and propaganda campaigns to achieve their ends.

They realize that if they can divide our national will at home, it will not be necessary to defeat our forces abroad. So by presenting issues in bellicose terms, they aim to intimidate western leaders and citizens, encouraging us to adopt conciliatory positions to their advantage. Meanwhile they remain sheltered from the force of public opinion in their countries, because public opinion there is simply prohibited and does not exist.

Our freedom presents both a challenge and an opportunity. It is true that until democratic nations do not have the support of the people, they are inevitably at a disadvantage in a conflict.

But when they do have that support they cannot be defeated. For democracies have the power to send a compelling message to friend and foe alike by the vote of their citizens.

And the American people have sent such a signal by re-electing a strong Chief Executive. They know that President Reagan is willing to accept the responsibility for his actions and is able to lead us through these complex times by insisting that we regain both our military and our economic strength.

In today's world where minutes count, such decisive leadership is more important than ever before. Regardless of whether conflicts are limited, or threats are ill defined, we must be capable of quickly determining that the threats and conflicts either do or do not affect the vital interests of the United States and our allies....And then responding appropriately.

Those threats may not entail an immediate, direct attack on our territory, and our response may not necessarily require the immediate or direct defense of our homeland.

But when our vital national interests and those of our allies are at stake, we cannot ignore our safety, or forsake our allies. At the same time, recent history has proven that we cannot assume unilaterally the role of the world's defender. We have learned that there are limits to how much of our spirit and blood and treasure we can afford to forfeit in meeting our responsibility to keep peace and freedom. So while we may and should offer substantial amounts of economic and military assistance to our allies in their time of need, and help them maintain forces to deter attacks against them usually we cannot substitute our troops or our will for theirs.

We should only engage our troops if we must do so as a matter of our own vital national interest. We cannot assume for other sovereign nations the responsibility to defend their territory without their strong invitation when our freedom is not threatened.

On the other hand, there have been recent cases where the United States has seen the need to join forces with other nations to try to preserve the peace by helping with negotiations, and by separating warring parties, and thus enabling those warring nations to withdraw from hostilities safely. In the Middle East, which has been torn by conflict for millennia, we have sent our troops in recent years both to the Sinai and to Lebanon, for just such a peacekeeping mission. But we did not configure or equip those forces for combat they were armed only for their self-defense. Their mission required them to be and to be recognized as peacekeepers. We knew that if conditions deteriorated so they were in danger, or if because of the actions of the warring nations, their peacekeeping mission could not be realized, then it would be necessary either to add sufficiently to the number and arms of our troops in short to equip them for combat ... or to withdraw them.

And so in Lebanon, when we faced just such a choice, because the warring nations did not enter into withdrawal or peace agreements, the President properly withdrew forces equipped only for peacekeeping.

In those cases where our national interests require us to commit combat force we must never let there be doubt of our resolution. When it is necessary for our troops to be committed to combat, we must commit them, in sufficient numbers and we must support them, as effectively and resolutely as our strength permits. When we commit our troops to combat we must do so with the sole object of winning.

Once it is clear our troops are required, because our vital interests are at stake, then we must have the firm national resolve to commit every ounce of strength necessary to win the fight to achieve our objectives. In Grenada we did just that.

Just as clearly, there are other situations where United States combat forces should not be used. I believe the postwar period has taught us several lessons, and from them I have developed six major tests to be applied when we are weighing the use of US combat forces abroad. Let me now share them with you:

(1) First, the United States should not commit forces to combat overseas unless the particular engagement or occasion is deemed vital to our national interest or that of our allies. That emphatically does not mean that we should declare beforehand, as we did with Korea in 1950, that a particular area is outside our strategic perimeter.

(2) Second, if we decide it is necessary to put combat troops into a given situation, we should do so wholeheartedly, and with the clear intention of winning. If we are unwilling to commit the forces or resources necessary to achieve our objectives, we should not commit them at all. Of course if the particular situation requires only limited force to win our objectives, then we should not hesitate to commit forces sized accordingly. When Hitler broke treaties and remilitarized the Rhineland, small combat forces then could perhaps have prevented the holocaust of World War II.

(3) Third, if we do decide to commit forces to combat overseas, we should have clearly defined political and military objectives. And we should know precisely how our forces can accomplish those clearly defined objectives. And we should have and send the forces needed to do just that. As Clausewitz wrote, "no one starts a war or rather, no one in his senses ought to do so without first being clear in his mind what he intends to achieve by that war, and how he intends to conduct it."

War may be different today than in Clausewitz's time, but the need for well-defined objectives and a consistent strategy is still essential. If we determine that a combat mission has become necessary for our vital national interests, then we must send forces capable to do the job and not assign a combat mission to a force configured for peacekeeping.

(4) Fourth, the relationship between our objectives and the forces we have committed their size, composition and disposition must be continually reassessed and adjusted if necessary. Conditions and objectives invariably change during the course of a conflict. When they do change, then so must our combat requirements. We must continuously keep as a beacon light before us the basic questions: "Is this conflict in our national interest?" "Does our national interest require us to fight, to use force of arms?" If the answers are "yes," then we must win. If the answers are "no," then we should not be in combat.

(5) Fifth, before the U.S. commits combat forces abroad, there must be some reasonable assurance we will have the support of the American people and their elected representatives in Congress. This support cannot be achieved unless we are candid in making clear the threats we face; the support cannot be sustained without continuing and close consultation. We cannot fight a battle with the Congress at home while asking our troops to win a war overseas or, as in the case of Vietnam, in effect asking our troops not to win, but just to be there.

(6) Finally, the commitment of U.S. forces to combat should be a last resort.

I believe that these tests can be helpful in deciding whether or not we should commit our troops to combat in the months and years ahead. The point we must all keep uppermost in our minds is that if we ever decide to commit forces to combat, we must support those forces to the fullest extent of our national will for as long as it takes to win. So we must have in mind objectives that are clearly defined and understood and supported by the widest possible number of our citizens. And those objectives must be vital to our survival as a free nation and to the fulfillment of our responsibilities as a world power. We must also be farsighted enough to sense when immediate and strong reactions to apparently small events can prevent lion-like responses that may be required later. We must never forget those isolationists in Europe who shrugged that "Dazing is not worth a war," and "why should we fight to keep the Rhineland demilitarized?"

These tests I have just mentioned have been phrased negatively for a purpose they are intended to sound a note of caution that we must observe prior to committing forces to combat overseas. When we ask our military forces to risk their very lives in such situations, a note of caution is not only prudent, it is morally required.

In many situations we may apply these tests and conclude that a combatant role is not appropriate. Yet no one should interpret what I am saying here today as an abdication of America's responsibilities either to its own citizens or to its allies. Nor should these remarks be misread as a signal that this country, or this Administration, is unwilling to commit forces to combat overseas.

We have demonstrated in the past that, when our vital interests or those of our allies are threatened, we are ready to use force, and use it decisively, to protect those interests.

Let no one entertain any illusions if our vital interests are involved, we are prepared to fight. And we are resolved that if we must fight, we must win.

So, while these tests are drawn from lessons we have learned from the past, they also can and should be applied to the future. For example, the problems confronting us in Central America today are difficult. The possibility of more extensive Soviet and Soviet proxy penetration into this hemisphere in months ahead is something we should recognize. If this happens we will clearly need more economic and military assistance and training to help those who want democracy.

The President will not allow our military forces to creep or be drawn gradually into a combat role in Central America or any other place in the world. And indeed our policy is designed to prevent the need for direct American involvement. This means we will need sustained Congressional support to back and give confidence to our friends in the region.

I believe that the tests I have enunciated here today can, if applied carefully, avoid the danger of this gradualist incremental approach, which almost always means the use of insufficient force. These tests can help us to avoid being drawn inexorably into an endless morass, where it is not vital to our national interest to fight.

But policies and principles such as these require decisive leadership in both the Executive and Legislative branches of government and they also require strong and sustained public support. Most of all, these policies require national unity of purpose. I believe the United States now possesses the policies and leadership to gain that public support and unity. And I believe that the future will show we have the strength of character to protect peace with freedom.

In summary, we should all remember these are the policies indeed the only policies that can preserve for ourselves, our friends, and our posterity, peace with freedom.

9
REMARKS BY PRESIDENT BILL CLINTON ON FOREIGN POLICY[30]

February 26, 1999
Grand Hyatt Hotel, San Francisco, California

The President: Thank you and good morning. Mr. Mayor, we're delighted to be here in San Francisco. We thank you for coming out to welcome us. Senator Boxer, Representative Pelosi, Representative Lofgren, members of the California legislature who are here. I'd like to especially thank two people who had a lot to do with the good things that have happened in the last six years in our administration, our former Secretary of Defense Bill Perry, and Mrs. Perry, are here; and General John Shalikashvili, thank you for coming. We're delighted to see you. (*Applause*)

I very much appreciate this opportunity to speak with all of you, to be joined with Secretary Albright and Mr. Berger, to talk about America's role in that century to come; to talk about what we must do to realize the promise of this extraordinary moment in the history of the world. For the first time since before the rise of fascism early in this century, there is no overriding threat to our survival or our freedom.

---

[30] www.**mtholyoke.edu**/acad/intrel/clintfps.htm

Perhaps for the first time in history, the world's leading nations are not engaged in a struggle with each other for security or territory. The world clearly is coming together.

Since 1945, global trade has grown fifteen-fold, raising living standards on every continent. Freedom is expanding; for the first time in history, more than half the world's people elect their own leaders. Access to information by ordinary people the world over is literally exploding.

Because of these developments, and the dramatic increase in our own prosperity and confidence in this, the longest peacetime economic expansion in our history, the United States has the opportunity and, I would argue, the solemn responsibility to shape a more peaceful, prosperous, democratic world in the twenty-first century.

We must, however, begin this discussion with a little history and a little humility. Listen to this quote by another American leader, at the dawn of a new century: "The world's products are exchanged as never before, and with increasing transportation comes increasing knowledge and larger trade. We travel greater distances in a shorter space of time, and with more ease, than was ever dreamed of. The same important news is read, though in different languages, the same day, in all the world. Isolation is no longer possible. No nation can longer be indifferent to any other."

That was said by President William McKinley a hundred years ago. What we now call globalization was well underway even then. We, in fact, had more diplomatic posts in the world than we have today, and foreign investment actually played a larger role in our own economy then than it does today.

The optimism being expressed about the twentieth century by President McKinley and others at that time was not all that much different from the hopes commonly expressed today about the twenty-first. The rising global trade and communications did lift countless lives then, just as it does today. But it did not stop the world's wealthiest nations from waging World War I and World War II. It did not stop the Depression, or the Holocaust, or communism. Had leading nations acted decisively then, perhaps these disasters might have been prevented. But the League of Nations failed, and America—well, our principal involvement in the world was commercial and cultural, unless and until we were attacked.

After World War II, our leaders took a different course. Harry Truman came to this city and said that to change the world away from a world in which might makes right, "words are not enough. We must once and for all prove by our acts conclusively that right has might." He and his allies and their successors built a network of security alliances to preserve the peace, and a global financial system to preserve prosperity. Over the last six years, we have been striving to renew those arrangements and to create new ones for the challenges of the next fifty years. We have made progress, but there is so very much more to do. We cannot assume today that globalization alone will wash away the forces of destruction at the dawn of the twenty-first century, any more than it did at the dawn of the twentieth century. We cannot assume it will bring freedom and prosperity to ordinary citizens around the world who long for them. We cannot assume it will assume it will avoid environmental and public health disasters. We cannot assume that because we are now secure, we Americans do not need military strength or alliances, or that because we are prosperous, we are not vulnerable to financial turmoil half a world away.

The world we want to leave our children and grandchildren requires us to make the right choices, and some of them will be difficult. America has always risen to great causes, yet we have a tendency, still, to believe that we can go back to minding our own business when we're done. Today we must embrace the inexorable logic of globalization—that everything, from the strength of our economy to the safety of our cities, to the health of our people, depends on events not only within our borders, but half a world away. We must see the opportunities and the dangers of the interdependent world in which we are clearly fated to live.

There is still the potential for major regional wars that would threaten our security. The arms race between India and Pakistan reminds us that the next big war could still be nuclear. There is a risk that our former adversaries will not succeed in their transitions to freedom and free markets. There is a danger that deadly weapons will fall into the hands of a terrorist group or an outlaw nation, and that those weapons could be chemical or biological.

There is a danger of deadly alliances among terrorists, narco-traffickers, and organized criminal groups. There is a danger of global environmental crises and the spread of deadly diseases. There is a danger that global financial turmoil will undermine open markets, overwhelm open societies, and undercut our own prosperity.

We must avoid both the temptation to minimize these dangers, and the illusion that the proper response to them is to batten down the hatches and protect America against the world. The promise of our future lies in the world. Therefore, we must work hard with the world—to defeat the dangers we face together and to build this hopeful moment together, into a generation of peace, prosperity, and freedom. Because of our unique position, America must lead with confidence in our strengths and with a clear vision of what we seek to avoid and what we seek to advance.

Our first challenge is to build a more peaceful twenty-first century world. To that end, we're renewing alliances that extend the area where wars do not happen, and working to stop the conflicts that are claiming lives and threatening our interests right now.

The century's bloodiest wars began in Europe. That's why I've worked hard to build a Europe that finally is undivided, democratic and at peace. We want all of Europe to have what America helped build in Western Europe—a community that upholds common standards of human rights, where people have the confidence and security to invest in the future, where nations cooperate to make war unthinkable.

That is why I have pushed hard for NATO's enlargement and why we must keep NATO's doors open to new democratic members, so that other nations will have an incentive to deepen their democracies. That is why we must forge a partnership between NATO and Russia, between NATO and Ukraine; why we are building a NATO capable not only of deterring aggression against its own territory, but of meeting challenges to our security beyond its territory—the kind of NATO we must advance at the fiftieth Anniversary Summit in Washington this April.

We are building a stronger alliance with Japan, and renewing our commitment to deter aggression in Korea and intensifying our efforts for a genuine peace there. I thank Secretary Perry for his efforts in that regard. We also create a more peaceful world by building new partnerships in Asia, Africa, and Latin America.

Ten years ago we were shouting at each other across a North–South chasm defined by our differences. Today, we are engaged in a new dialogue that speaks the language of common interests—of trade and investment; of education and health; of democracies that deliver not corruption and despair, but progress and hope; of a common desire that children in all our countries will be free of the scourge of drugs. Through these efforts to strengthen old alliances and build new partnerships, we advance the prospects for peace. However, the work of actually making peace is harder and often far more contentious.

It's easy, for example, to say that we really have no interests in who lives in this or that valley in Bosnia, or who owns a strip of brushland in the Horn of Africa, or some piece of parched earth by the Jordan River. But the true measure of our interests lies not in how small or distant these places are, or in whether we have trouble pronouncing their names. The question we must ask is, what are the consequences to our security of letting conflicts fester and spread. We cannot, indeed, we should not, do everything or be everywhere. But where are values and our interests are at stake, and where we can make a difference, we must be prepared to do so. And we must remember that the real challenge of foreign policy is to deal with problems before they harm our national interests.

It's also easy to say that peacemaking is simply doomed, where people are embittered by generations of hate, where the old animosities of race and religion and ethnic difference raise their hoary heads. But I will never forget the day that the leaders of Israel and the Palestinian Authority came to the White House, in September of 1993, to sign their peace accord. At that moment, the question arose, and indeed, based on the pictures afterward, it seemed to be the main question, whether if, in front of the entire world, Prime Minister Rabin and Chairman Arafat would actually shake hands for the first time.

It was an interesting and occasionally humorous discussion. But it ended when Yitzhak Rabin, a soldier for a lifetime, said to me, "Mr. President, I have been fighting this man for a lifetime, thirty years. I have buried a lot of my own people in the process. But you do not make peace with your friends."

It is in our interest to be a peacemaker, not because we think we can make all these differences go away, but because, in over two hundred years of hard effort here at home, and with bitter and good experiences around the world, we have learned that the world works better when differences are resolved by the force of argument rather than the force of arms.

That is why I am proud of the work we have done to support peace in Northern Ireland, and why we will keep pressing the leaders there to observe not just the letter, but the spirit of the Good Friday Accord. (*Applause*)

It is also why I intend to use the time I have remaining in this office to push for a comprehensive peace in the Middle East, to encourage Israelis and Palestinians to reach a just and final settlement, and to stand by our friends for peace, such as Jordan. The people of the Middle East can do it, but time is precious, and they can't afford to waste any more of it. In their hearts, they know there can be no security or justice for any who live in that small and sacred land until there is security and justice for all who live there. If they do their part, we must do ours.

We will also keep working with our allies to build peace in the Balkans. Three years ago, we helped to end the war in Bosnia. A lot of doubters then thought it would soon start again. But Bosnia is on a steady path toward renewal and democracy. We've been able to reduce our troops there by 75 percent as peace has taken hold, and we will continue to bring them home.

The biggest remaining danger to this progress has been the fighting and the repression in Kosovo. Kosovo is, after all, where the violence in the former Yugoslavia began, over a decade ago, when they lost the autonomy guaranteed under Yugoslav law. We have a clear national interest in ensuring that Kosovo is where this trouble ends. If it continues, it almost certainly will draw in Albania and Macedonia, which share borders with Kosovo, and on which clashes have already occurred.

Potentially, it could affect our allies, Greece and Turkey. It could spark tensions in Bosnia itself, jeopardizing the gains made there. If the conflict continues, there will certainly be more atrocities, more refugees, more victims crying out for justice and seeking out revenge.

Last fall, a quarter of a million displaced people in Bosnia were facing cold and hunger in the hills. Using diplomacy backed by force, we brought them home and slowed the fighting.

For seventeen days this month, outside Paris, we sought with our European partners an agreement that would end the fighting for good. Progress was made toward a common understanding of Kosovo's autonomy—progress that would not have happened, I want to say, but for the unity of our allies and the tireless leadership of our Secretary of State Madeleine Albright. (*Applause*)

Here's where we are. Kosovar Albanian leaders have agreed in principle to a plan that would protect the rights of their people and give them substantial self-government. Serbia has agreed to much, but not all, of the conditions of autonomy, and has so far not agreed to the necessity of a NATO-led international force to maintain the peace there.

Serbia's leaders must now accept that only by allowing people in Kosovo control over their day-to-day lives—as, after all, they have been promised under Yugoslav law—it is only by doing that can they keep their country intact. Both sides must return to the negotiations on March 15, with clear mandate for peace. In the meantime, President Milosevic should understand that this is a time for restraint, not repression. And if he does not, NATO is prepared to act.

Now, if there is a peace agreement that is effective, NATO must also be ready to deploy to Kosovo to give both sides the confidence to lay down their arms. Europeans would provide the great bulk of such a force, roughly 85 percent. But if there is a real peace, America must do its part as well.

Kosovo is not an easy problem. But if we don't stop the conflict now, it clearly will spread. And then we will not be able to stop it, except at far greater cost and risk.

A second challenge we face is to bring our former adversaries, Russia and China, into the international system as open, prosperous, stable nations. The way both countries develop in the coming century will have a lot to do with the future of our planet.

For fifty years, we confronted the challenge of Russia's strength. Today, we must confront the risk of a Russia weakened by the legacy of communism and also by its inability at the moment to maintain prosperity at home or control the flow of its money, weapons and technology across its borders.

The dimensions of this problem are truly enormous. Eight years after the Soviet collapse, the Russian people are hurting. The economy is shrinking, making the future uncertain. Yet, we have as much of a stake today in Russia overcoming these challenges as we did in checking its expansion during the Cold War. This is not a time for complacency or self-fulfilling pessimism. Let's not forget that Russia's people have overcome enormous obstacles before. And just this decade, with no living memory of democracy or freedom to guide them, they have built a country more open to the world than ever; a country with a free press and a robust, even raucous debate; a country that should see in the first year of the new millennium the first peaceful democratic transfer of power in its thousand-year history.

The Russian people will decide their own future. But we must work with them for the best possible outcome, with realism and with patience. If Russia does what it must to make its economy work, I am ready to do everything I can to mobilize adequate international support for them. With the right framework, we will also encourage foreign investment in its factories, its energy fields, its people. We will increase our support for small business and for the independent media. We will work to continue cutting our two nations' nuclear arsenals, and help Russia prevent both its weapons and its expertise from falling into the wrong hands.

The budget I have presented to Congress will increase funding for this critical threat reduction by 70 percent over the next five years.

The question China faces is how best to assure its stability and progress. Will it choose openness and engagement? Or will it choose to limit the aspirations of its people without fully embracing the global rules of the road? In my judgment, only the first path can really answer the challenges China faces.

We cannot minimize them. China has made incredible progress in lifting people out of poverty, and building a new economy. But now its rate of economic growth is declining—just as it is needed to create jobs for a growing, and increasingly more mobile, population. Most of China's economy is still stifled by state control. We can see in China the kinds of problems a society faces when it is moving away from the rule of fear, but is not yet rooted in the rule of law.

China's leaders know more economic reform is needed, and they know reform will cause more unemployment, and they know that can cause unrest. At the same time, and perhaps for those reasons, they remain unwilling to open up their political system, to give people a peaceful outlet for dissent.

Now, we Americans know that dissent is not always comfortable, not always easy, and often raucous. But I believe that the fact that we have peaceful, orderly outlets for dissent is one of the principal reasons we're still around here as the longest-lasting freely elected government in the world. And I believe, sooner or later, China will have to come to understand that a society, in the world we're living in—particularly a country as great and old and rich and full of potential as China—simply cannot purchase stability at the expense of freedom.

On the other hand, we have to ask ourselves, what is the best thing to do to try to maximize the chance that China will take the right course, and that, because of that, the world will be freer, more peaceful, more prosperous in the twenty-first century? I do not believe we can hope to bring change to China if we isolate China from the forces of change. Of course, we have our differences, and we must press them. But we can do that, and expand our cooperation, through principled and purposeful engagement with China, its government, and its people.

Our third great challenge is to build a future in which our people are safe from the dangers that arise, perhaps halfway around the world—dangers from proliferation, from terrorism, from drugs, from the multiple catastrophes that could arise from climate change.

Each generation faces the challenges of not trying to fight the last war. In our case, that means recognizing that the more likely future threat to our existence is not a strategic nuclear strike from Russia or China, but the use of weapons of mass destruction by an outlaw nation or a terrorist group.

In the last six years, fighting that threat has become a central priority of American foreign policy. Here, too, there is much more to be done. We are working to stop weapons from spreading at the source, as with Russia. We are working to keep Iraq in check so that it does not threaten the rest of the world or its region with weapons of mass destruction. We are using all the means at our disposal to deny terrorists safe havens, weapons, and funds. Even if it takes years, terrorists must know there is no place to hide.

Recently, we tracked down the gunman who killed two of our people outside the CIA six years ago. We are training and equipping our local fire, police and medical personnel to deal with chemical, biological and nuclear emergencies, and improving our public health surveillance system, so that if a biological weapon is released, we can detect it and save lives. We are working to protect our critical computer systems from sabotage.

Many of these subjects are new and unfamiliar, and may be frightening. As I said when I gave an address in Washington not very long ago about what we were doing on biological and computer security and criminal threats, it is important that we have the right attitude about this. It is important that we understand that the risks are real and they require, therefore, neither denial, nor panic. As long as people organize themselves in human societies, there will be organized forces of destruction who seek to take advantage of new means of destroying other people.

And the whole history of conflict can be seen in part as the race of defensive measures to catch up with offensive capabilities. That is what we're doing in dealing with the computer challenges today; that is what we are doing in dealing with the biological challenges today. It is very important that the American people, without panic, be serious and deliberate about them, because it is the kind of challenge that we have faced repeatedly. And as long as our country and the world is around, unless there is some completely unforeseen change in human nature, our successors will have to do the same.

We are working to develop a national missile defense system which could, if we decide to deploy it, be deployed against emerging ballistic missile threats from rogue nations. We are bolstering the global agreements that curb proliferation. That's the most important thing we can be doing right now. This year, we hope to achieve an accord to strengthen compliance with the Convention against Biological Weapons. It's a perfectly good convention, but, frankly, it has no teeth. We have to give it some. And we will ask our Senate to ratify the Comprehensive Test Ban Treaty to stop nations from testing nuclear weapons so they're constrained from developing new ones.

Again, I say: I implore the United States Senate to ratify the Comprehensive Test Ban Treaty this year. It is very important for the United States and the world. (*Applause*)

Our security and our safety also depends upon doing more to protect our people from the scourge of drugs. To win this fight, we must work with others, including and especially Mexico. Mexico has a serious drug problem, increasingly affecting more of its own young people. No one understands this better than President Zedillo. He described it as the number one threat to his country's security, its people its democracy. He is working hard to establish clean government, true democracy and the rule of law. He is working hard to tackle the corruption traffickers have wrought.

He cannot win this battle alone, and neither can we. In any given year, the narco-traffickers may spend hundreds of millions of dollars to try to suborn Mexican law enforcement officials, most of whom work for under $10,000 a year.

As I certified to Congress today, Mexico is cooperating with us in the battle for our lives. And I believe the American people will be safer in this, as in so many other ways, if we fight drugs with Mexico, rather than walk away.

Another global danger we face is climate change. As far as we can tell, with all the scientific evidence available, the hottest years our planet has ever experienced were 1997 and 1998. The two hottest years recorded in the last several—excuse me—nine of the ten hottest years recorded in the last several centuries occurred in the last decade.

Now, we can wait and hope and do nothing, and try to ignore what the vast majority of scientists tell us is a pattern that is fixed and continuing. We could ignore the record-breaking temperatures, the floods, the storms, the droughts that have caused such misery. Or we can accept that preventing the disease and destruction climate change can bring will be infinitely cheaper than letting future generations try to clean up the mess, especially when you consider that greenhouse gases, once emitted into the atmosphere, last and have a destructive environmental effect for at least a hundred years.

We took a giant step forward in 1997, when we helped to forge the Kyoto agreement. Now we're working to persuade developing countries that they, too, can and must participate meaningfully in this effort without forgoing growth. We are also trying to persuade a majority in the United States Congress that we can do the same thing.

The approach I have taken in America is not to rely on a whole raft of new regulations, and not to propose big energy taxes, but instead to offer tax incentives and dramatic increases in investment in new technologies, because we know—we know now—that we have the technological capacity to break the iron link between Industrial Age energy use patterns and economic growth. You're proving it in California every day, with stiffer environmental standards than other states have.

We know that the technology is just beginning to emerge to allow us to have clean cars and other clean forms of transportation; to dramatically increase the capacity of all of our buildings to keep out heat and cold, and to let in more light. We know that the conservation potential of what we have right now available has only just been scratched. And we must convince the world, and critical decision makers in the United States to change their minds about a big idea—namely, that the only way a country can grow is to consume more energy resources in a way that does more to increase global warning.

One of the most interesting conversations I had when I was in China was with the Environmental Minister there, who thanked me for going there to do an environmental event, because he was having trouble convincing the government that they could continue to lift the Chinese people out of poverty and still improve the environment. This is a central, big idea that people all over the world will have to change their minds about before we will be open and free to embrace the technological advances that are lying evident all around us. And all of you that can have any impact on that, I implore you to do it. (*Applause*)

Our fourth challenge is to create a world trading and financial system that will lift the lives of ordinary people on every continent around the world. Or, as it has been stated in other places, to put a human face on the global economy. Over the last six years, we've taken giant steps in opening the global trading system. The United States alone has concluded over 270 different trade agreements. Once again, we are the world's largest exporting nation. There is a lot more to be done.

In the first five years of my presidency, about 30 percent of our growth came from expanding trade. Last year, we had a good year, but we didn't have much growth from expanding trade because of the terrible difficulties of the people in Asia, in Russia, and because of the slowdown in growth in Latin America, and because we did not reach out to seize new possibilities in Africa. Those people are suffering more, and our future prospects are being constrained.

The question is what to do about it. Some of the folks outside who were protesting when I drove up were saying by their signs that they believe globalization is inherently bad and there's no way in the wide world to put a human face on the global economy. But if you look at the facts of the last thirty years, hundreds of millions of people have had their economic prospects advanced on every continent because they have finally been able to find a way to express their creativity in positive terms, and produce goods and services that could be purchased around the borders of their nation.

Now, the question is, how do we deal with the evident challenges and problems that we face in high relief today, and seize the benefit that we know comes from expanding trade. I've asked for a new round of global trade negotiations to expand exports of services, foreign products and manufacturers. I am still determined to reach agreement on a free trade area of the Americas. If it hadn't been for our expansion in Latin America, from Mexico all the way to the southern tip of South America, we would have been in much worse shape this last year.

I have urged Congress to give the trade authority the President has traditionally had to advance our prosperity, and I've asked them to approve the Caribbean Basin Initiative and the Africa Growth and Opportunity Act because we have special responsibilities and special opportunities in the Caribbean and in Africa that have gone too long unseized.

But trade is not an end in itself. It has to work for ordinary people; it has to contribute to the wealth and fairness of societies. It has to reinforce the values that give meaning to life, not simply in the United States, but in the poorest countries, struggling to lift their people to their dreams. That's why we're working to build a trading system that upholds the rights of workers and consumers, and helps us and them in other countries to protect the environment, so that competition among nations is a race to the top, not the bottom. This year we will lead the international community to conclude a treaty to ban abusive child labor everywhere in the world. (*Applause*)

The gains of global economic exchange have been real and dramatic. But when the tides of capital first flood emerging markets, and then abruptly recede; when bank failures and bankruptcies grip entire economies; when millions who have worked their way into the middle class are plunged suddenly into poverty—the need for reform of the international financial system is clear.

I don't want to minimize the complexity of this challenge. As nations began to trade more, and as investment rules began to permit people to invest in countries other than their own more, it became more and more necessary to facilitate the conversion of currencies.

Whenever you do that, you will create a market against risk, just in the transfer of currencies. Whenever you do that, you will have people that are moving money around because they think the value of the money itself will change, and profit might be gained in an independent market of currency exchange.

It is now true that on any given day, there is $1.5 trillion of currency exchange in the world. Many, many, many times more than the actual value of the exchange of goods and services. And we have got to find a way to facilitate the movement of money—without which trade and investment cannot occur—in a way that avoids these dramatic cycles of boom and then bust, which have led to the collapse of economic activity in so many countries around the world.

We found a way to do it in the United States after the Great Depression. And thank goodness we have never again had a Great Depression, even though we've had good times and bad times. That is the challenge facing the world financial system today.

The leading economies have got a lot of work to do. We have to do everything we can—not just the United States, but Europe and Japan—to spur economic growth. Unless there is a restoration of growth, all the changes in the financial rules we make will not get Asia, Latin America countries— Russia—out of their difficulties.

We have to be ready to provide quick and decisive help to nations committed to sound policies. We have to help nations build social safety nets so that, when they have inevitable changes in their economic conditions, people at least have the basic security they need to continue to embrace change and advance the overall welfare of society.

We have to encourage nations to maintain open, properly regulated financial systems so that decisions are shaped by informed market decisions and not distorted by corruption. We also have to take responsible steps to reform the global financial architecture for the twenty-first century. And we'll do some more of that at the G-7 summit in Germany in June.

In the meanwhile, we have to recognize that the United States has made a great contribution to keeping this crisis from being worse than it would have been by helping to get money to Brazil, to Russia, to other countries, and by keeping our own markets open. If you compare, for example, our import patterns with those of Europe or those of

Japan, you will see that we have far, far more open markets. It has worked to make us competitive and productive. We also have the lowest unemployment rate in the entire world among all advanced countries now, something that many people thought would never happen again.

On the other hand, we cannot let other countries' difficulties in our open markets become an excuse for them to violate international trade rules and dump products illegally on our markets. We've had enough problems in America this year and last year—in agriculture and aerospace, especially—from countries that could no longer afford to buy products, many of which they had already offered. Then, in the last several months, we've seen an enormous problem in this country in our steel industry because of evident dumping of products in the American market that violated the law.

So I want you to know what while I will do everything to keep our markets open, I intend while this crisis persists to do everything I can to enforce our trade laws.

Yesterday, we received some evidence that our aggressive policy is producing some results, and I think proof that it wasn't market forces that led to what we saw in steel over the last year. The new figures from the Commerce Department show this: Imports of hot-rolled steel from countries most responsible for the surge—Japan, Russia and Brazil—have fallen by 96 percent from the record levels we saw last November.

That is not bad news for them, that's good news. If American markets are going to stay open, we have to play by the rules. We have to follow lawful economic trends, not political and economic decisions made to dump on the American markets in ways which hurt our economy and undermine our ability to buy the exports of other countries.

Our fifth challenge has to keep freedom as a top goal for the world of the twenty-first century. Countries like South Korea and Thailand have proven in this financial crisis that open societies are more resilient, that elected governments have a legitimacy to make hard choices in hard times. But if democracies over the long run aren't able to deliver for their people, to take them out of economic turmoil, the pendulum that swung so decisively toward freedom over the last few years could swing back, and the next century could begin as badly as this one began in that regard.

Therefore, beyond economics, beyond the transformation of the great countries to economic security—Russia and China—beyond many of our security concerns, we also have to recognize that we can have no greater purpose than to support the right of other people to live in freedom and shape their own destiny. If that right could be universally exercised, virtually every goal I have outlined today would be advanced.

We have to keep standing by those who risk their own freedom to win it for others. Today we're releasing our annual Human Rights Report: The message of the Human Rights Report is often resented, but always respected, for its candor, its consistency for what it says about our country and our values. We need to deepen democracy where it's already taking root by helping our partners narrow their income gaps, strengthen their legal institutions, and build well-educated, healthy societies.

This will be an important part of the trip I take to Central America next week, which has prevailed against decades of civil war only to be crushed in the last several months by the devastating force of nature.

This year, we will see profoundly important developments in the potential transition to democracy in two critical countries—Indonesia and Nigeria. Both have the capacity to lift their entire regions if they succeed, and to swamp them in a sea of disorder if they fail. In the coming year and beyond, we must make a concentrated effort to help them achieve what will be the world's biggest victories for freedom since 1989.

Nigeria is the most populous country in Africa. Tomorrow, it holds its first free presidential election, after a dictatorship that made it the poorest oil-rich country in the world. We are providing support for the transition, and if it succeeds we have to be prepared to do more. Because we count on further progress, today we are also waiving the sanctions we imposed when its government did not cooperate in the fight against drugs.

Indonesia is the fourth-largest nation and the largest Islamic country in the entire world. In June, it will hold what we hope will be its first truly democratic election in more than forty years. Indonesia desperately needs a government that can help it overcome its economic crisis while maintaining the support of its people. We are helping to strengthen the social safety net for its people in providing the largest contribution of any nation to support the coming elections.

Whether these struggles are far or near, their outcome will profoundly affect us. Whether a child in Africa or Southeast Asia or Russia or China can grow up educated, healthy, safe, free from violence, free of hate, full of hope, and free to decide his or her own destiny, this will have a lot to do with the life our children have as they grow up. It will help to determine if our children go to war, have jobs, have clean air, have safe streets.

For our nation to be strong, we must maintain a consensus that seemingly distant problems can come home if they are not addressed, and addressed promptly. We must recognize we cannot lift ourselves to the heights to which we aspire if the world is not rising with us. I say again, the inexorable logic of globalization is the genuine recognition of interdependence. We cannot wish into being the world we seek. Talk is cheap; decisions are not.

That is why I have asked Congress to reverse the decline in defense spending that began in 1985, and I am hopeful and confident that we can get bipartisan majorities in both Houses to agree. I hope it will also agree to give more support to our diplomats, and to programs that keep our soldiers out of war; to fund assistance programs to keep nations on a stable path to democracy and growth; and to finally pay both our dues and our debts to the United Nations. (*Applause*)

In an interdependent world, we cannot lead if we expect to lead only on our own terms, and never on our own nickel. We can't be a first-class power if we're only prepared to pay for steerage.

I hope all of you, as citizens, believe that we have to seize the responsibilities that we have today with confidence—to keep taking risks for peace; to keep forging opportunities for our people, and seeking them for others as well; to seek to put a genuinely human face on the global economy; to keep faith with all those around the world who struggle for human rights, the rule of law, a better life; to look on our leadership not as a burden, but as a welcome opportunity; to build the future we dream for our children in these, the final days of the twentieth century, and the coming dawn of the next.

The story of the twenty-first century can be quite a wonderful story. But we have to write the first chapter. Thank you very much. (*Applause*)

10

REBUILDING AMERICA'S DEFENSES: STRATEGY, FORCES, AND RESOURCES FOR A NEW CENTURY[31]

A Report of the Project for the New American Century, September 2000

INTRODUCTION

The Project for the New American Century was established in the spring of 1997. From its inception, the Project has been concerned with the decline in the strength of America's defenses, and in the problems this would create for the exercise of American leadership around the globe and, ultimately, for the preservation of peace.

---

[31] This document is so important that it should be studied separately. It offers a radical new philosophy and constitutes a letter of intent presenting a new vision of America in the twenty-first century.
www.**informationclearinghouse.info**/pdf/RebuildingAmericasDefenses.pdf

Our concerns were reinforced by the two congressionally-mandated defense studies that appeared soon thereafter: the Pentagon's Quadrennial Defense Review (May 1997) and the report of the National Defense Panel (December 1997). Both studies assumed that U.S. defense budgets would remain flat or continue to shrink. As a result, the defense plans and recommendations outlined in the two reports were fashioned with such budget constraints in mind. Broadly speaking, the QDR stressed current military requirements at the expense of future defense needs, while the NDP's report emphasized future needs by underestimating today's defense responsibilities.

Although the QDR and the report of the NDP proposed different policies, they shared one underlying feature: the gap between resources and strategy should be resolved not by increasing resources but by shortchanging strategy. America's armed forces, it seemed, could either prepare for the future by retreating from its role as the essential defender of today's global security order, or it could take care of current business but be unprepared for tomorrow's threats and tomorrow's battlefields.

Either alternative seemed to us shortsighted. The United States is the world's only superpower, combining preeminent military power, global technological leadership, and the world's largest economy. Moreover, America stands at the head of a system of alliances which includes the world's other leading democratic powers. At present the United States faces no global rival. America's grand strategy should aim to preserve and extend this advantageous position as far into the future as possible. There are, however, potentially powerful states dissatisfied with the current situation and eager to change it, if they can, in directions that endanger the relatively peaceful, prosperous and free condition the world enjoys today. Up to now, they have been deterred from doing so by the capability and global presence of American military power. But, as that power declines, relatively and absolutely, the happy conditions that follow from it will be inevitably undermined.

Preserving the desirable strategic situation in which the United States now finds itself requires a globally preeminent military capability both today and in the future. But years of cuts in defense spending have eroded the American military's combat readiness, and put in jeopardy the Pentagon's plans for maintaining military superiority in the years ahead. Increasingly, the U.S. military has found itself undermanned, inadequately equipped and trained, straining to handle contingency operations, and ill-prepared to adapt itself to the revolution in military affairs. Without a well-conceived defense policy and an appropriate increase in defense spending, the United States has been letting its ability to take full advantage of the remarkable strategic opportunity at hand slip away.

With this in mind, we began a project in the spring of 1998 to examine the country's defense plans and resource requirements. We started from the premise that U.S. military capabilities should be sufficient to support an American grand strategy committed to building upon this unprecedented opportunity. We did not accept pre-ordained constraints that followed from assumptions about what the country might or might not be willing to expend on its defenses.

At present the United States faces no global rival. America's grand strategy should aim to preserve and extend this advantageous position as far into the future as possible.

In broad terms, we saw the project as building upon the defense strategy outlined by the Cheney Defense Department in the waning days of the Bush Administration. The Defense Policy Guidance (DPG) drafted in the early months of 1992 provided a blueprint for maintaining U.S. preeminence, precluding the rise of a great power rival, and shaping the international security order in line with American principles and interests. Leaked before it had been formally approved, the document was criticized as an effort by "cold warriors" to keep defense spending high and cuts in forces small despite the collapse of the Soviet Union; not surprisingly, it was subsequently buried by the new administration.

Although the experience of the past eight years has modified our understanding of particular military requirements for carrying out such a strategy, the basic tenets of the DPG, in our judgment, remain sound. And what Secretary Cheney said at the time in response to the DPG's critics remains true today: "We can either sustain the [armed] forces we require and remain in a position to help shape things for the better, or we can throw that advantage away. [But] that would only hasten the day when we face greater threats, at higher costs and further risk to American lives."

The project proceeded by holding a series of seminars. We asked outstanding defense specialists to write papers to explore a variety of topics: the future missions and requirements of the individual military services, the role of the reserves, nuclear strategic doctrine and missile defenses, the defense budget and prospects for military modernization, the state (training and readiness) of today's forces, the revolution in military affairs, and defense-planning for theater wars, small wars and constabulary operations. The papers were circulated to a group of participants, chosen for their experience and judgment in defense affairs. (The list of participants may be found at the end of this report.) Each paper then became the basis for discussion and debate. Our goal was to use the papers to assist deliberation, to generate and test ideas, and to assist us in developing our final report. While each paper took as its starting point a shared strategic point of view, we made no attempt to dictate the views or direction of the individual papers. We wanted as full and as diverse a discussion as possible.

Our report borrows heavily from those deliberations. But we did not ask seminar participants to "sign-off" on the final report. We wanted frank discussions and we sought to avoid the pitfalls of trying to produce a consensual but bland product. We wanted to try to define and describe a defense strategy that is honest, thoughtful, bold, internally consistent and clear. And we wanted to spark a serious and informed discussion, the essential first step for reaching sound conclusions and for gaining public support.

New circumstances make us think that the report might have a more receptive audience now than in recent years. For the first time since the late 1960s the federal government is running a surplus. For most of the 1990s, Congress and the White House gave balancing the federal budget a higher priority than funding national security. In fact, to a significant degree, the budget was balanced by a combination of increased tax revenues and cuts in defense spending. The surplus expected in federal revenues over the next decade, however, removes any need to hold defense spending to some preconceived low level.

Moreover, the American public and its elected representatives have become increasingly aware of the declining state of the U.S. military. News stories, Pentagon reports, congressional testimony and anecdotal accounts from members of the armed services paint a disturbing picture of an American military that is troubled by poor enlistment and retention rates, shoddy housing, a shortage of spare parts and weapons, and diminishing combat readiness.

Finally, this report comes after a decade's worth of experience in dealing with the post-Cold War world. Previous efforts to fashion a defense strategy that would make sense for today's security environment were forced to work from many untested assumptions about the nature of a world without a superpower rival. We have a much better idea today of what our responsibilities are, what the threats to us might be in this new security environment, and what it will take to secure the relative peace and stability. We believe our report reflects and benefits from that decade's worth of experience.

Our report is published in a presidential election year. The new administration will need to produce a second Quadrennial Defense Review shortly after it takes office. We hope that the Project's report will be useful as a road map for the nation's immediate and future defense plans. We believe we have set forth a defense program that is justified by the evidence, rests on an honest examination of the problems and possibilities, and does not flinch from facing the true cost of security. We hope it will inspire careful consideration and serious discussion. The post–Cold War world will not remain a relatively peaceful place if we continue to neglect foreign and defense matters. But serious attention, careful thought, and the willingness to devote adequate resources to maintaining America's military strength can make the world safer and American strategic interests more secure now and in the future.

Donald Kagan and **Gary Schmitt,**
Project Co-Chairmen

Thomas Donnelly,
Principal Author

KEY FINDINGS

This report proceeds from the belief that America should seek to preserve and extend its position of global leadership by maintaining the preeminence of U.S. military forces. Today, the United States has an unprecedented strategic opportunity. It faces no immediate great-power challenge; it is blessed with wealthy, powerful and democratic allies in every part of the world; it is in the midst of the longest economic expansion in its history; and its political and economic principles are almost universally embraced. At no time in history has the international security order been as conducive to American interests and ideals. The challenge for the coming century is to preserve and enhance this "American peace."

Yet unless the United States maintains sufficient military strength, this opportunity will be lost. And in fact, over the past decade, the failure to establish a security strategy responsive to new realities and to provide adequate resources for the full range of missions needed to exercise U.S. global leadership has placed the American peace at growing risk. This report attempts to define those requirements.

In particular, we need to:

ESTABLISH FOUR CORE MISSIONS for U.S. military forces:
- defend the American homeland;
- fight and decisively win multiple, simultaneous major theater wars;
- perform the "constabulary" duties associated with shaping the security environment in critical regions;
- transform U.S. forces to exploit the "revolution in military affairs;"

To carry out these core missions, we need to provide sufficient force and budgetary allocations. In particular, the United States must:

MAINTAIN NUCLEAR STRATEGIC SUPERIORITY, basing the U.S. nuclear deterrent upon a global, nuclear net assessment that weighs the full range of current and emerging threats, not merely the U.S.-Russia balance.

RESTORE THE PERSONNEL STRENGTH of today's force to roughly the levels anticipated in the "Base Force" outlined by the Bush Administration, an increase in active-duty strength from 1.4 million to 1.6 million.

REPOSITION U.S. FORCES to respond to 21st century strategic realities by shifting permanently-based forces to Southeast Europe and Southeast Asia, and by changing naval deployment patterns to reflect growing U.S. strategic concerns in East Asia.

MODERNIZE CURRENT U.S. FORCES SELECTIVELY, proceeding with the F-22 program while increasing purchases of lift, electronic support and other aircraft; expanding submarine and surface combatant fleets; purchasing Comanche helicopters and medium-weight ground vehicles for the Army, and the V-22 Osprey "tilt-rotor" aircraft for the Marine Corps.

CANCEL "ROADBLOCK" PROGRAMS such as the Joint Strike Fighter, CVX aircraft carrier, and Crusader howitzer system that would absorb exorbitant amounts of Pentagon funding while providing limited improvements to current capabilities. Savings from these canceled programs should be used to spur the process of military transformation.

DEVELOP AND DEPLOY GLOBAL MISSILE DEFENSES to defend the American homeland and American allies, and to provide a secure basis for U.S. power projection around the world.

CONTROL THE NEW "INTERNATIONAL COMMONS" OF SPACE AND "CYBERSPACE," and pave the way for the creation of a new military service – U.S. Space Forces – with the mission of space control.

EXPLOIT THE "REVOLUTION IN MILITARY AFFAIRS" to insure the long-term superiority of U.S. conventional forces. Establish a two-stage transformation process which
- maximizes the value of current weapons systems through the application of advanced technologies, and,

- produces more profound improvements in military capabilities, encourages competition between single services and joint-service experimentation efforts.

INCREASE DEFENSE SPENDING gradually to a minimum level of 3.5 to 3.8 percent of gross domestic product, adding $15 billion to $20 billion to total defense spending annually.

Fulfilling these requirements is essential if America is to retain its militarily dominant status for the coming decades. Conversely, the failure to meet any of these needs must result in some form of strategic retreat. At current levels of defense spending, the only option is to try ineffectually to "manage" increasingly large risks: paying for today's needs by shortchanging tomorrow's; withdrawing from constabulary missions to retain strength for large-scale wars; "choosing" between presence in Europe or presence in Asia; and so on. These are bad choices. They are also false economies.

The "savings" from withdrawing from the Balkans, for example, will not free up anywhere near the magnitude of funds needed for military modernization or transformation. But these are false economies in other, more profound ways as well. The true cost of not meeting our defense requirements will be a lessened capacity for American global leadership and, ultimately, the loss of a global security order that is uniquely friendly to American principles and prosperity.

I -Why Another Defense Review?

Since the end of the Cold War, the United States has struggled to formulate a coherent national security or military strategy, one that accounts for the constants of American power and principles yet accommodates 21st century realities. Absent a strategic framework, U.S. defense planning has been an empty and increasingly self-referential exercise, often dominated by bureaucratic and budgetary rather than strategic interests. Indeed, the proliferation of defense reviews over the past decade testifies to the failure to chart a consistent course: to date, there have been half a dozen formal defense reviews, and the Pentagon is now gearing up for a second Quadrennial Defense

Review in 2001. Unless this "QDR II" matches U.S. military forces and resources to a viable American strategy, it, too, will fail.

These failures are not without cost: already, they place at risk an historic opportunity. After the victories of the past century—two world wars, the Cold War and most recently the Gulf War—the United States finds itself as the uniquely powerful leader of a coalition of free and prosperous states that faces no immediate great-power challenge.

The American peace has proven itself peaceful, stable and durable. It has, over the past decade, provided the geopolitical framework for widespread economic growth and the spread of American principles of liberty and democracy. Yet no moment in international politics can be frozen in time; even a global *Pax Americana* will not preserve itself.

Paradoxically, as American power and influence are at their apogee, American military forces limp toward exhaustion, unable to meet the demands of their many and varied missions, including preparing for tomorrow's battlefield. Today's force, reduced by a third or more over the past decade, suffers from degraded combat readiness; from difficulties in recruiting and retaining sufficient numbers of soldiers, sailors, airmen and Marines; from the effects of an extended "procurement holiday" that has resulted in the premature aging of most weapons systems; from an increasingly obsolescent and inadequate military infrastructure; from a shrinking industrial base poorly structured to be the "arsenal of democracy" for the 21st century; from a lack of innovation that threatens the technological and operational advantages enjoyed by U.S. forces for a generation and upon which American strategy depends. Finally, and most dangerously, the social fabric of the military is frayed and worn. U.S. armed forces suffer from a degraded quality of life divorced from middle-class expectations, upon which an all-volunteer force depends. Enlisted men and women and junior officers increasingly lack confidence in their senior leaders, whom they believe will not tell unpleasant truths to their civilian leaders. In sum, as the American peace reaches across the globe, the force that preserves that peace is increasingly overwhelmed by its tasks.

This is no paradox; it is the inevitable consequence of the failure to match military means to geopolitical ends. Underlying the failed strategic and defense reviews of the past decade is the idea that the collapse of the Soviet Union had created a "strategic pause." In other words, until another great power challenger emerges, the United States can enjoy a respite from the demands of international leadership. Like a boxer between championship bouts, America can afford to relax and live the good life, certain that there would be enough time to shape up for the next big challenge. Thus the United States could afford to reduce its military forces, close bases overseas, halt major weapons programs and reap the financial benefits of the "peace dividend." But as we have seen over the past decade, there has been no shortage of powers around the world who have taken the collapse of the Soviet empire as an opportunity to expand their own influence and challenge the American-led security order.

Beyond the faulty notion of a strategic pause, recent defense reviews have suffered from an inverted understanding of the military dimension of the Cold War struggle between the United States and the Soviet Union. American containment strategy did not proceed from the assumption that the Cold War would be a purely military struggle, in which the U.S. Army matched the Red Army tank for tank; rather, the United States would seek to deter the Soviets militarily while defeating them economically and ideologically over time. And, even within the realm of military affairs, the practice of deterrence allowed for what in military terms is called "an economy of force." The principle job of NATO forces, for example, was to deter an invasion of Western Europe, not to invade and occupy the Russian heartland. Moreover, the bipolar nuclear balance of terror made both the United States and the Soviet Union generally cautious. Behind the smallest proxy war in the most remote region lurked the possibility of Armageddon. Thus, despite numerous miscalculations through the five decades of Cold War, the United States reaped an extraordinary measure of global security and stability simply by building a credible and, in relative terms, inexpensive nuclear arsenal.

Over the decade of the post-Cold-War period, however, almost everything has changed. The Cold War world was a bipolar world; the 21st century world is—for the moment, at least— decidedly unipolar, with America as the world's "sole superpower." America's strategic goal used to be containment of the Soviet Union; today the task is to preserve an international security environment conducive to American interests and ideals. The military's job during the Cold War was to deter Soviet expansionism. Today its task is to secure and expand the "zones of democratic peace;" to deter the rise of a new great power competitor; defend key regions of Europe, East Asia and the Middle East; and to preserve American preeminence through the coming transformation of war made possible by new technologies.

Cold War and 21st Century
Security system
Bipolar, Unipolar

Strategic goal
Contain Soviet Union, Preserve *Pax Americana*

Main military mission(s)
Deter Soviet expansionism, Secure and expand zones of democratic peace; deter rise of new great-power competitor; defend key regions; exploit transformation of war

Main military threat(s)
Potential global war across many theaters. Potential theater wars spread across globe

Focus of strategic competition
Europe, East Asia

Today, America spends less than 3 percent of its gross domestic product on national defense, less than at any time since before the United States established itself as the world's leading power.

From 1945 to 1990, U.S. forces prepared themselves for a single, global war that might be fought across many theaters; in the new century, the prospect is for a variety of theater wars around the world, against separate and distinct adversaries pursuing separate and distinct goals. During the Cold War, the main venue of superpower rivalry, the strategic "center of gravity," was in Europe, where large U.S. and NATO conventional forces prepared to repulse a Soviet attack and over which nuclear war might begin; and with Europe now generally at peace, the new strategic center of concern appears to be shifting to East Asia. The missions for America's armed forces have not diminished so much as shifted. The threats may not be as great, but there are more of them. During the Cold War, America acquired its security "wholesale" by global deterrence of the Soviet Union. Today, that same security can only be acquired at the "retail" level, by deterring or, when needed, by compelling regional foes to act in ways that protect American interests and principles.

This gap between a diverse and expansive set of new strategic realities and diminishing defense forces and resources does much to explain why the Joint Chiefs of Staff routinely declare that they see "high risk" in executing the missions assigned to U.S. armed forces under the government's declared national military strategy. Indeed, a JCS assessment conducted at the height of the Kosovo air war found the risk level "unacceptable." Such risks are the result of the combination of the new missions described above and the dramatically reduced military force that has emerged from the defense "drawdown" of the past decade. Today, America spends less than 3 percent of its gross domestic product on national defense, less than at any time since before World War II—in other words, since before the United States established itself as the world's leading power—and a cut from 4.7 percent of GDP in 1992, the first real post-Cold-War defense budget. Most of this reduction has come under the Clinton Administration; despite initial promises to approximate the level of defense spending called for in the final Bush Administration program, President Clinton cut more than $160 billion from the Bush program from 1992 to 1996 alone. Over the first seven years of the Clinton Administration, approximately $426 billion in defense investments have been deferred, creating a weapons procurement "bow wave" of immense proportions.

The most immediate effect of reduced defense spending has been a precipitate decline in combat readiness. Across all services, units are reporting degraded readiness, spare parts and personnel shortages, postponed and simplified training regimens, and many other problems. In congressional testimony, service chiefs of staff now routinely report that their forces are inadequate to the demands of the "two war" national military strategy. Press attention focused on these readiness problems when it was revealed that two Army divisions were given a "C-4" rating, meaning they were not ready for war. Yet it was perhaps more telling that *none* of the Army's ten divisions achieved the highest "C-1" rating, reflecting the widespread effects of slipping readiness standards. By contrast, *every* division that deployed to Operation Desert Storm in 1990 and 1991 received a "C-1" rating. This is just a snapshot that captures the state of U.S. armed forces today. These readiness problems are exacerbated by the fact that U.S. forces are poorly positioned to respond to today's crises. In Europe, for example, the overwhelming majority of Army and Air Force units remain at their Cold War bases in Germany or England, while the security problems on the continent have moved to Southeast Europe. Temporary rotations of forces to the Balkans and elsewhere in Southeast Europe increase the overall burdens of these operations many times. Likewise, the Clinton Administration has continued the fiction that the operations of American forces in the Persian Gulf are merely temporary duties. Nearly a decade after the Gulf War, U.S. air, ground and naval forces continue to protect enduring American interests in the region. In addition to rotational naval forces, the Army maintains what amounts to an armored brigade in Kuwait for nine months of every year; the Air Force has two composite air wings in constant "no-fly zone" operations over northern and southern Iraq. And despite increasing worries about the rise of China and instability in Southeast Asia, U.S. forces are found almost exclusively in Northeast Asian bases.

Yet for all its problems in carrying out today's missions, the Pentagon has done almost nothing to prepare for a future that promises to be very different and potentially much more dangerous. It is now commonly understood that information and other new technologies—as well as widespread technological and weapons proliferation—are creating a dynamic that may threaten America's ability to exercise its dominant military power. Potential rivals such as China are anxious to exploit these transformational technologies broadly, while adversaries like Iran, Iraq and North Korea are rushing to develop ballistic missiles and nuclear weapons as a deterrent to American intervention in regions they seek to dominate. Yet the Defense Department and the services have done little more than affix a "transformation" label to programs developed during the Cold War, while diverting effort and attention to a process of joint experimentation which restricts rather than encourages innovation. Rather than admit that rapid technological changes makes it uncertain which new weapons systems to develop, the armed services cling ever more tightly to traditional program and concepts. As Andrew Krepinevich, a member of the National Defense

Panel, put it in a recent study of Pentagon experimentation, "Unfortunately, the Defense Department's rhetoric asserting the need for military transformation and its support for joint experimentation has yet to be matched by any great sense of urgency or any substantial resource support.... At present the Department's effort is poorly focused and woefully underfunded."

In sum, the 1990s have been a "decade of defense neglect." This leaves the next president of the United States with an enormous challenge: he must increase military spending to preserve American geopolitical leadership, or he must pull back from the security commitments that are the measure of America's position as the world's sole superpower and the final guarantee of security, democratic freedoms and individual political rights. This choice will be among the first to confront the president: new legislation requires the incoming administration to fashion a national security strategy within six months of assuming office, as opposed to waiting a full year, and to complete another quadrennial defense review three months after that. In a larger sense, the new president will choose whether today's "unipolar moment," to use columnist Charles Krauthammer's phrase for America's current geopolitical preeminence, will be extended along with the peace and prosperity that it provides.

This study seeks to frame these choices clearly, and to re-establish the links between U.S. foreign policy, security strategy, force planning and defense spending. If an American peace is to be maintained, and expanded, it must have a secure foundation on unquestioned U.S. military preeminence.

II - FOUR ESSENTIAL MISSIONS

America's global leadership, and its role as the guarantor of the current great-power peace, relies upon the safety of the American homeland; the preservation of a favorable balance of power in Europe, the Middle East and surrounding energy producing region, and East Asia; and the general stability of the international system of nation-states relative to terrorists, organized crime, and other "non-state actors." The relative importance of these elements, and the threats to U.S. interests, may rise and fall over time. Europe, for example, is now extraordinarily peaceful and stable, despite the turmoil in the Balkans. Conversely, East Asia appears to be entering a period with increased potential for instability and competition. In the Gulf, American power and presence has achieved relative external security for U.S. allies, but the longer-term prospects are murkier.

Generally, American strategy for the coming decades should seek to consolidate the great victories won in the 20th century—which have made Germany and Japan into stable democracies, for example—maintain stability in the Middle East, while setting the conditions for 21st-century successes, especially in East Asia.

None of the defense reviews of the past decade has weighed fully the range of missions demanded by U.S. global leadership, nor adequately quantified the forces and resources necessary to execute these missions successfully.

A retreat from any one of these requirements would call America's status as the world's leading power into question. As we have seen, even a small failure like that in Somalia or a halting and incomplete triumph as in the Balkans can cast doubt on American credibility. The failure to define a coherent global security and military strategy during the post-Cold-War period has invited challenges; states seeking to establish regional hegemony continue to probe for the limits of the American security perimeter. None of the defense reviews of the past decade has weighed fully the range of missions demanded by U.S. global leadership: defending the homeland, fighting and winning multiple large-scale wars, conducting constabulary missions which preserve the current peace, and transforming the U.S. armed forces to exploit the "revolution in military affairs."

Nor have they adequately quantified the forces and resources necessary to execute these missions separately and successfully. While much further detailed analysis would be required, it is the purpose of this study to outline the large, "full spectrum" forces that are necessary to conduct the varied tasks demanded by a strategy of American preeminence for today and tomorrow.

HOMELAND DEFENSE. America must defend its homeland. During the Cold War, nuclear deterrence was the key element in homeland defense; it remains essential. But the new century has brought with it new challenges. While reconfiguring its nuclear force, the United States also must counteract the effects of the proliferation of ballistic missiles and weapons of mass destruction that may soon allow lesser states to deter U.S. military action by threatening U.S. allies and the American homeland itself. Of all the new and current missions for U.S. armed forces, this must have priority.

LARGE WARS. Second, the United States must retain sufficient forces able to rapidly deploy and win multiple simultaneous large-scale wars and also to be able to respond to unanticipated contingencies in regions where it does not maintain forward-based forces.

This resembles the "two-war" standard that has been the basis of U.S. force planning over the past decade. Yet this standard needs to be updated to account for new realities and potential new conflicts.

CONSTABULARY DUTIES. Third, the Pentagon must retain forces to preserve the current peace in ways that fall short of conduction major theater campaigns. A decade's experience and the policies of two administrations have shown that such forces must be expanded to meet the needs of the new, long-term NATO mission in the Balkans, the continuing no-fly-zone and other missions in Southwest Asia, and other presence missions in vital regions of East Asia. These duties are today's most frequent missions, requiring forces configured for combat but capable of long-term, independent constabulary operations.

TRANSFORM U.S. ARMED FORCES. Finally, the Pentagon must begin now to exploit the so called "revolution in military affairs," sparked by the introduction of advanced technologies into military systems; this must be regarded as a separate and critical mission worthy of a share of force structure and defense budgets.

Current American armed forces are ill prepared to execute these four missions. Over the past decade, efforts to design and build effective missile defenses have been ill-conceived and underfunded, and the Clinton Administration has proposed deep reductions in U.S. nuclear forces without sufficient analysis of the changing global nuclear balance of forces. While, broadly speaking, the United States now maintains sufficient active and reserve forces to meet the traditional two-war standard, this is true only in the abstract, under the most favorable geopolitical conditions. As the Joint Chiefs of Staff have admitted repeatedly in congressional testimony, they lack the forces necessary to meet the two-war benchmark as expressed in the war-plans of the regional commanders-in-chief. The requirements for major-war forces must be reevaluated to accommodate new strategic realities. One of these new realities is the requirement for peacekeeping operations; unless this requirement is better understood, America's ability to fight major wars will be jeopardized. Likewise, the transformation process has gotten short shrift.

To meet the requirements of the four new missions highlighted above, the United States must undertake a two-stage process. The immediate task is to rebuild today's force, ensuring that it is equal to the tasks before it: shaping the peacetime environment and winning multiple, simultaneous theater wars; these forces must be large enough to accomplish these tasks without running the "high" or "unacceptable" risks it faces now. The second task is to seriously embark upon a transformation of the Defense Department. This itself will be a two-stage effort: for the next decade or more, the armed forces will continue to operate many of the same systems it now does, organize themselves in traditional units, and employ current operational concepts.

A new assessment of the global nuclear balance, one that takes account of Chinese and other nuclear forces as well as Russian, must precede decisions about U.S. nuclear force cuts.

However, this transition period must be a first step toward more substantial reform. Over the next several decades, the United States must field a global system of missile defenses, divine ways to control the new "international commons" of space and cyberspace, and build new kinds of conventional forces for different strategic challenges and a new technological environment.

Nuclear Forces

Current conventional wisdom about strategic forces in the post-Cold-War world is captured in a comment made by the late Les Aspin, the Clinton Administration's first secretary of defense. Aspin wrote that the collapse of the Soviet Union had "literally reversed U.S. interests in nuclear weapons" and, "Today, if offered the magic wand to eradicate the existence and knowledge of nuclear weapons, we would very likely accept it." Since the United States is the world's dominant conventional military power, this sentiment is understandable. But it is precisely because we have such power that smaller adversarial states, looking for an equalizing advantage, are determined to acquire their own weapons of mass destruction. Whatever our fondest wishes, the reality of the today's world is that there is no magic wand with which to eliminate these weapons (or, more fundamentally, the interest in acquiring them) and that deterring their use requires a reliable and dominant U.S. nuclear capability.

While the formal U.S. nuclear posture has remained conservative through the 1994 Nuclear Posture Review and the 1997 Quadrennial Defense Review, and senior Pentagon leaders speak of the continuing need for nuclear deterrent forces, the Clinton Administration has taken repeated steps to undermine the readiness and effectiveness of U.S. nuclear forces. In particular, it has virtually ceased development of safer and more effective nuclear weapons; brought underground testing to a complete halt; and allowed the Department of Energy's weapons complex and associated scientific expertise to atrophy for lack of support. The administration has also made the decision to retain current weapons in the active force for years beyond their design life. When combined with the decision to cut back on regular, non-nuclear flight and system tests of the weapons themselves, this raises a host of questions about the continuing safety and reliability of the nation's strategic arsenal. The administration's stewardship of the nation's deterrent capability has been aptly described by Congress as "erosion by design."

A new assessment of the global nuclear balance, one that takes account of Chinese and other nuclear forces as well as Russian, must precede decisions about U.S. nuclear force cuts.

Rather than maintain and improve America's nuclear deterrent, the Clinton Administration has put its faith in new arms control measures, most notably by signing the Comprehensive Test Ban Treaty (CTBT). The treaty proposed a new multilateral regime, consisting of some 150 states, whose principal effect would be to constrain America's unique role in providing the global nuclear umbrella that helps to keep states like Japan and South Korea from developing the weapons that are well within their scientific capability, while doing little to stem nuclear weapons proliferation. Although the Senate refused to ratify the treaty, the administration continues to abide make sense to continue the current moratorium on nuclear testing for the moment—since it would take a number of years to refurbish the neglected testing infrastructure in any case—ultimately this is an untenable situation. If the United States is to have a nuclear deterrent that is both effective and safe, it will need to test.

The administration's stewardship of the nation's deterrent capability has been described by Congress as "erosion by design."

That said, of all the elements of U.S. military force posture, perhaps none is more in need of reevaluation than America's nuclear weapons. Nuclear weapons remain a critical component of American military power but it is unclear whether the current U.S. nuclear arsenal is well-suited to the emerging post-Cold War world. Today's strategic calculus encompasses more factors than just the balance of terror between the United States and Russia. U.S. nuclear force planning and related arms control policies must take account of a larger set of variables than in the past, including the growing number of small nuclear arsenals—from North Korea to Pakistan to, perhaps soon, Iran and Iraq—and a modernized and expanded Chinese nuclear force. Moreover, there is a question about the role nuclear weapons should play in deterring the use of other kinds of weapons of mass destruction, such as chemical and biological, with the U.S. having foresworn those weapons' development and use. It addition, there may be a need to develop a new family of nuclear weapons designed to address new sets of military requirements, such as would be required in targeting the very deep underground, hardened bunkers that are being built by many of our potential adversaries. Nor has there been a serious analysis done of the benefits versus the costs of maintaining the traditional nuclear "triad." What is needed first is a global net assessment of what kinds and numbers of nuclear weapons the U.S. needs to meet its security responsibilities in a post-Soviet world.

In short, until the Department of Defense can better define future its nuclear requirements, significant reductions in U.S. nuclear forces might well have unforeseen consequences that lessen rather than enhance the security of the United States and its allies. Reductions, upon review, might be called for. But what should finally drive the size and character of our nuclear forces is not numerical parity with Russian capabilities but maintaining American strategic superiority—and, with that superiority, a capability to deter possible hostile coalitions of nuclear powers. U.S. nuclear superiority is nothing to be ashamed of; rather, it will be an essential element in preserving American leadership in a more complex and chaotic world.

Forces for Major Theater Wars

The one constant of Pentagon force planning through the past decade has been the recognized need to retain sufficient combat forces to fight and win, as rapidly and decisively as possible, multiple, nearly simultaneous major theater wars. This constant is based upon two important truths about the current international order. One, the Cold-War standoff between America and its allies and the Soviet Union that made for caution and discouraged direct aggression against the major security interests of either side no longer exists. Two, conventional warfare remains a viable way for aggressive states to seek major changes in the international order.

Iraq's 1990 invasion of Kuwait reflected both truths. The invasion would have been highly unlikely, if not impossible, within the context of the Cold War, and Iraq overran Kuwait in a matter of hours. These two truths revealed a third: maintaining or restoring a favorable order in vital regions in the world such as Europe, the Middle East and East Asia places a unique responsibility on U.S. armed forces.

The Gulf War and indeed the subsequent lesser wars in the Balkans could hardly have been fought and won without the dominant role played by American military might. Thus, the understanding that U.S. armed forces should be shaped by a "two-major-war" standard rightly has been accepted as the core of America's superpower status since the end of the Cold War. The logic of past defense reviews still obtains, and received its clear exposition in the 1997 Quadrennial Defense Review, which argued:

A force sized and equipped for deterring and defeating aggression in more than one theater ensures that the United States will maintain the flexibility to cope with the unpredictable and unexpected. Such a capability is the sine qua non of a superpower and is essential to the credibility of our overall national security strategy....If the
United States were to forego its ability to defeat aggression in more than one theater at a time, our standing as a global power, as the security partner of choice and the leader of the international community would be called in to question. Indeed, some allies would undoubtedly read a one-war capability as a signal that the United States, if heavily engaged elsewhere, would no longer be able to defend their interests...A one-theater-war capacity would risk undermining ... the credibility of U.S. security commitments in key regions of the world. This, in turn, could cause allies and friends to adopt more divergent defense policies and postures, thereby weakening the web of alliances and coalitions on which we rely to protect our interests abroad.

In short, anything less than a clear two-war capacity threatens to devolve into a no-war strategy. Unfortunately, Defense Department thinking about this requirement was frozen in the early 1990s. The experience of Operation Allied Force in the Balkans suggests that, if anything, the canonical two-war force-sizing standard is more likely to be too low than too high. The Kosovo air campaign eventually involved the level of forces anticipated for a major war, but in a theater other than the two – the Korean peninsula and Southwest Asia—that have generated past Pentagon planning scenarios. Moreover, new theater wars that can be foreseen, such as an American defense of Taiwan against a Chinese invasion or punitive attack, have yet to be formally considered by Pentagon planners.

The Joint Chiefs have admitted they lack the forces necessary to meet the two-war benchmark.

To better judge forces needed for building an American peace, the Pentagon needs to begin to calculate the force necessary to protect, independently, U.S. interests in Europe, East Asia and the Gulf at all times. The actions of our adversaries in these regions bear no more than a tangential relationship to one another; it is more likely that one of these regional powers will seize an opening created by deployments of U.S. forces elsewhere to make mischief.

Thus, the major-theater-war standard should remain the principal force-sizing tool for U.S. conventional forces. This not to say that this measure has been perfectly applied in the past: Pentagon analyses have been both too optimistic and too pessimistic, by turns. For example, the analyses done of the requirement to defeat an Iraqi invasion of Kuwait and Saudi Arabia almost certainly overestimates the level of force required. Conversely, past analyses of a defense of South Korea may have underestimated the difficulties of such a war, especially if North Korea employed weapons of mass destruction, as intelligence estimates anticipate.

Moreover, the theater-war analysis done for the QDR assumed that Kim Jong Il and Saddam Hussein each could begin a war—perhaps even while employing chemical, biological or even nuclear weapons—and the United States would make no effort to unseat militarily either ruler. In both cases, past Pentagon war-games have given little or no consideration to the force requirements necessary not only to defeat an attack but to remove these regimes from power and conduct post-combat stability operations. In short, past Defense Department application of the two-war standard is not a reliable guide to the real force requirements— and, of course, past reviews included no analysis of the kind of campaign in Europe as was seen in Operation Allied Force. Because past Pentagon strategy reviews have been budget-driven exercises, it will be necessary to conduct fresh and more realistic analyses even of the canonical two-war scenarios.

In sum, while retaining the spirit of past force-planning for major wars, the Department of Defense must undertake a more nuanced and thoroughgoing review of real requirements. The truths that gave rise to the original two-war standard endure: America's adversaries will continue to resist the building of the American peace; when they see an opportunity as Saddam Hussein did in 1990, they will employ their most powerful armed forces to win on the battlefield what they could not win in peaceful competition; and American armed forces will remain the core of efforts to deter, defeat, or remove from power regional aggressors.

Forces for 'Constabulary' Duties

In addition to improving the analysis needed to quantify the requirements for major theater wars, the Pentagon also must come to grips with the real requirements for constabulary missions. The 1997 Quadrennial Defense Review rightly acknowledged that these missions, which it dubbed "smaller-scale contingencies," or SSCs, would be the frequent and unavoidable diet for U.S. armed forces for many years to come: "Based on recent experience and intelligence projections, the demand for SSC operations is expected to remain high over the next 15 to 20 years," the review concluded. Yet, at the same time, the QDR failed to allocate any forces to these missions, continuing the fiction that, for force planning purposes, constabulary missions could be considered "lesser included cases" of major theater war requirements. "U.S. forces must also be able to withdraw from SSC operations, reconstitute, and then deploy to a major theater war in accordance with required timelines," the review argued.

The increasing number of 'constabulary' missions for U.S. troops, such as in Kosovo above, must be considered an integral element in Pentagon force planning.

The shortcomings of this approach were underscored by the experience of Operation Allied Force in the Balkans. Precisely because the forces engaged there would not have been able to withdraw, reconstitute and redeploy to another operation—and because the operation consumed such a large part of overall Air Force aircraft—the Joint Chiefs of Staff concluded that the United States was running "unacceptable" risk in the event of war elsewhere. Thus, facing up to the realities of multiple constabulary missions will require a permanent allocation of U.S. armed forces.

Nor can the problem be solved by simply withdrawing from current constabulary missions or by vowing to avoid them in the future. Indeed, withdrawing from today's ongoing missions would be problematic. Although the no-fly-zone air operations over northern and southern Iraq have continued without pause for almost a decade, they remain an essential element in U.S. strategy and force posture in the Persian Gulf region. Ending these operations would hand Saddam Hussein an important victory, something any American leader would be loath to do. Likewise, withdrawing from the Balkans would place American leadership in Europe—indeed, the viability of NATO—in question. While none of these operations involves a mortal threat, they do engage U.S. national security interests directly, as well as engaging American moral interests.

Further, these constabulary missions are far more complex and likely to generate violence than traditional "peacekeeping" missions. For one, they demand American political leadership rather than that of the United Nations, as the failure of the UN mission in the Balkans and the relative success of NATO operations there attests. Nor can the United States assume a UN-like stance of neutrality; the preponderance of American power is so great and its global interests so wide that it cannot pretend to be indifferent to the political outcome in the Balkans, the Persian Gulf or even when it deploys forces in Africa. Finally, these missions demand forces basically configured for combat. While they also demand personnel with special language, logistics and other support skills, the first order of business in missions such as in the Balkans is to establish security, stability and order. American troops, in particular, must be regarded as part of an overwhelmingly powerful force.

With a decade's worth of experience both of the requirements for current constabulary missions and with the chaotic political environment of the post-Cold War era, the Defense Department is more than able to conduct a useful assessment to quantify the overall needs for forces engaged in constabulary duties. While part of the solution lies in repositioning existing forces, there is no escaping the conclusion that these new missions, unforeseen when the defense drawdown began a decade ago, require an increase in overall personnel strength and U.S. force structure.

Transformation Forces

The fourth element in American force posture—and certainly the one which holds the key to any longer-term hopes to extend the current *Pax Americana*—is the mission to transform U.S. military forces to meet new geopolitical and technological challenges. While the prime directive for transformation will be to design and deploy a global missile defense system, the effects of information and other advanced technologies promise to revolutionize the nature of conventional armed forces. Moreover, the need to create weapons systems optimized for operations in the Pacific theater will create requirements quite distinct from the current generation of systems designed for warfare on the European continent and those new systems like the F-22 fighter that also were developed to meet late-Cold-War needs.

Although the basic concept for a system of global missile defenses capable of defending the United States and its allies against the threat of smaller and simpler ballistic missiles has been well understood since the late 1980s, a decade has been squandered in developing the requisite technologies. In fact, work on the key elements of such a system, especially those that would operate in space, has either been so slowed or halted completely, so that the process of deploying robust missile defenses remains a long-term project. If for no other reason, the mission to create such a missile defense system should be considered a matter of military transformation.

For the United States to retain the technological and tactical advantages it now enjoys, the transformation effort must be considered as pressing a military mission as preparing for today's theater wars.

As will be argued more fully below, effective ballistic missile defenses will be the central element in the exercise of American power and the projection of U.S. military forces abroad. Without it, weak states operating small arsenals of crude ballistic missiles, armed with basic nuclear warheads or other weapons of mass destruction, will be a in a strong position to deter the United States from using conventional force, no matter the technological or other advantages we may enjoy. Even if such enemies are merely able to threaten American allies rather than the United States homeland itself, America's ability to project power will be deeply compromised. Alas, neither Administration strategists nor Pentagon force planners seem to have grasped this elemental point; certainly, efforts to fund, design and develop an effective system of missile defenses do not reflect any sense of urgency. Nonetheless, the first task in transforming U.S. military to meet the technological and strategic realities of a new century is to create such a system.

Creating a system of global missile defenses is but the first task of transformation; the need to reshape U.S. conventional forces is almost as pressing. For, although American armed forces possess capabilities and enjoy advantages that far surpass those of even our richest and closest allies, let alone our declared and potential enemies, the combination of technological and strategic change that marks the new century places these advantages at risk. Today's U.S. conventional forces are masters of a mature paradigm of warfare, marked by the dominance of armored vehicles, aircraft carriers and, especially, manned tactical aircraft, that is beginning to be overtaken by a new paradigm, marked by long-range precision strikes and the proliferation of missile technologies. Ironically, it has been the United States that has pioneered this new form of high-technology conventional warfare: it was suggested by the 1991 Gulf War and has been revealed more fully by the operations of the past decade. Even the "Allied Force" air war for Kosovo showed a distorted version of the emerging paradigm of warfare.

Yet even these pioneering capabilities are the residue of investments first made in the mid- and late 1980s; over the past decade the pace of innovation within the Pentagon has slowed measurably. In part, this is due to reduced defense budgets, the overwhelming dominance of U.S. forces today, and the multiplicity of constabulary missions. And without the driving challenge of the Soviet military threat, efforts at innovation have lacked urgency. Nonetheless, a variety of new potential challenges can be clearly foreseen. The Chinese military, in particular, seeks to exploit the revolution in military affairs to offset American advantages in naval and air power, for example. If the United States is to retain the technological and tactical advantages it now enjoys in large-scale conventional conflicts, the effort at transformation must be considered as pressing a mission as preparing for today's potential theater wars or constabulary missions—indeed, it must receive a significant, separate allocation of forces and budgetary resources over the next two decades.

In addition, the process of transformation must proceed from an appreciation of American strategy and political goals. For example, as the leader of a global network of alliances and strategic partnerships, U.S. armed forces cannot retreat into a "Fortress America." Thus, while long-range precision strikes will certainly play an increasingly large role in U.S. military operations, American forces must remain deployed abroad, in large numbers. To remain as the leader of a variety of coalitions, the United States must partake in the risks its allies face; security guarantees that depend solely upon power projected from the continental United States will inevitably become discounted.

Moreover, the process of transformation should proceed in a spirit of competition among the services and between service and joint approaches. Inevitably, new technologies may create the need for entirely new military organizations; this report will argue below that the emergence of space as a key theater of war suggests forcefully that, in time, it may be wise to create a separate "space service." Thus far, the Defense Department has attempted to take a prematurely joint approach to transformation. While it is certain that new technologies will allow for the closer combination of traditional service capabilities, it is too early in the process of transformation to choke off what should be the healthy and competitive face of "interservice rivalry." Because the separate services are the military institutions most attuned to providing forces designed to carry out the specific missions required by U.S. strategy, they are in fact best equipped to become the engines of transformation and change within the context of enduring mission requirements.

Finally, it must be remembered that the process of transformation is indeed a process: even the most vivid view of the armed forces of the future must be grounded in an understanding of today's forces. In general terms, it seems likely that the process of transformation will take several decades and that U.S. forces will continue to operate many, if not most, of today's weapons systems for a decade or more. Thus, it can be foreseen that the process of transformation will in fact be a two-stage process: first of transition, then of more thoroughgoing transformation. The breakpoint will come when a preponderance of new weapons systems begins to enter service, perhaps when, for example, unmanned aerial vehicles begin to be as numerous as manned aircraft. In this regard, the Pentagon should be very wary of making large investments in new programs —tanks, planes, aircraft carriers, for example—that would commit U.S. forces to current paradigms of warfare for many decades to come.

In conclusion, it should be clear that these four essential missions for maintaining American military preeminence are quite separate and distinct from one another—none should be considered a "lesser included case" of another, even though they are closely related and may, in some cases, require similar sorts of forces. Conversely, the failure to provide sufficient forces to execute these four missions must result in problems for American strategy. The failure to build missile defenses will put America and her allies at grave risk and compromise the exercise of American power abroad. Conventional forces that are insufficient to fight multiple theater wars simultaneously cannot protect American global interests and allies. Neglect or withdrawal from constabulary missions will increase the likelihood of larger wars breaking out and encourage petty tyrants to defy American interests and ideals. And the failure to prepare for tomorrow's challenges will ensure that the current *Pax Americana* comes to an early end....

(This document is too long to be transcribed in its entirety. Therefore, only the first chapters are included as being relevant to the purpose of the discussion.)

Project Participants

Roger Barnett
U.S. Naval War College
Alvin Bernstein
National Defense University
Stephen Cambone
National Defense University
Eliot Cohen
Nitze School of Advanced International
Studies, Johns Hopkins University
Devon Gaffney Cross
Donors' Forum for International Affairs
Thomas Donnelly
Project for the New American Century
David Epstein
Office of Secretary of Defense,
Net Assessment
David Fautua
Lt. Col., U.S. Army
Dan Goure
Center for Strategic and International Studies
Donald Kagan
Yale University
Fred Kagan
U. S. Military Academy at West Point
Robert Kagan
Carnegie Endowment for International Peace
Robert Killebrew
Col., USA (Ret.)
William Kristol
The Weekly Standard
Mark Lagon
Senate Foreign Relations Committee
James Lasswell
GAMA Corporation

I. Lewis Libby
Dechert Price & Rhoads
Robert Martinage
Center for Strategic and Budgetary Assessment
Phil Meilinger
U.S. Naval War College
Mackubin Owens
U.S. Naval War College
Steve Rosen
Harvard University
Gary Schmitt
Project for the New American Century
Abram Shulsky
The RAND Corporation
Michael Vickers
Center for Strategic and Budgetary Assessment
Barry Watts
Northrop Grumman Corporation
Paul Wolfowitz
Nitze School of Advanced International Studies, Johns Hopkins University
Dov Zakheim
System Planning Corporation

The above list of individuals participated in at least one project meeting or contributed a paper for discussion. The report is a product solely of the Project for the New American Century and does not necessarily represent the views of the project participants or their affiliated institutions.

U.S. INTERVENTIONS IN LATIN AMERICA[32]

1846

Fulfilling the doctrine of Manifest Destiny, the United States goes to war with Mexico and ends up with a third of Mexico's territory.

1850, 1853, 1854, 1857

U.S. interventions in *Nicaragua*.

1855

Tennessee adventurer William Walker and his mercenaries take over Nicaragua, institute forced labor, and legalize slavery.
"Los yankis ... *have burst their way like a fertilizing torrent through the barriers of barbarism.*"—New York Daily News
Walker is ousted two years later by a Central American coalition largely inspired by Cornelius Vanderbilt, whose trade Walker was infringing.
"The enemies of American civilization—for such are the enemies of slavery—seem to be more on the alert than its friends."—William Walker

1856

First of five U.S. interventions in *Panama* to protect the Atlantic-Pacific railroad from Panamanian nationalists.

1898

U.S. declares war on *Spain*, blaming it for destruction of the USS *Maine*. (In 1976, a U.S. Navy commission will conclude that the explosion was probably an accident.) The war enables

---

[32] www.**zo**mpist.com/latam.html

the United States to occupy Cuba, Puerto Rico, Guam, and the Philippines.

1903

The Platt Amendment inserted into the *Cuban* constitution grants the United States the right to intervene when it sees fit.

1903

When negotiations with Colombia break down, the United States sends ten warships to back a rebellion in *Panama* in order to acquire the land for the Panama Canal. The Frenchman Philippe Bunau-Varilla negotiates the Canal Treaty and writes Panama's constitution.

1904

The United States sends customs agents to take over finances of the *Dominican Republic* to assure payment of its external debt.

1905

U.S. Marines help *Mexican* dictator Porfirio Díaz crush a strike in Sonora.

1905

U.S. troops land in *Honduras* for the first of five times in next twenty years.

1906

Marines occupy *Cuba* for two years in order to prevent a civil war.

1907

Marines intervene in *Honduras* to settle a war with Nicaragua.

1908

U.S. troops intervene in *Panama* for first of four times in next decade.

1909

Liberal President José Santos Zelaya of *Nicaragua* proposes that American mining and banana companies pay taxes; he has also appropriated church lands and legalized divorce, done business with European firms, and executed two Americans for participating in a rebellion. After he is forced through U.S. pressure to resign, the new president, Adolfo Díaz, is the former treasurer of an American mining company.

1910

U.S. Marines occupy *Nicaragua* to help support the Díaz regime.

1911

The Liberal regime of Miguel Dávila in *Honduras* has irked the State Department by being too friendly with Zelaya and by getting into debt with Britain. He is overthrown by former president Manuel Bonilla. Bonilla is aided by American banana tycoon Sam Zemurray and American mercenary Lee Christmas, who becomes commander-in-chief of the Honduran army.

1912

U.S. Marines intervene in *Cuba* to put down a rebellion of sugar workers.

1912

Nicaragua occupied again by the United States to shore up the inept Díaz government. An election is called to resolve the crisis: there are four thousand eligible voters, and one candidate, Díaz. The United States maintains troops and advisors in the country until 1925.

1914

The United States bombs and then occupies Vera Cruz in a conflict arising out of a dispute with *Mexico*'s new government. President Victoriano Huerta resigns.

1915

U.S. Marines occupy *Haiti* to restore order and establish a protectorate that lasts till 1934. The president of Haiti is barred from the U.S. Officers' Club in Port-au-Prince because he is black.
"Think of it—niggers speaking French!"
—*Secretary of State William Jennings Bryan when briefed on the Haitian situation*

1916

Marines occupy the *Dominican Republic*, staying until 1924.

1916

Pancho Villa, in the sole act of Latin American aggression against the United States, raids the city of Columbus, New Mexico, killing seventeen Americans.
"Am sure Villa's attacks are made in Germany."
—*James Gerard, U.S. ambassador to Berlin*

1917

U.S. troops enter *Mexico* to pursue Pancho Villa. They can't catch him.

1917

Marines intervene again in *Cuba*, to guarantee sugar exports during WWI.

1918

U.S. Marines occupy *Panamanian* province of Chiriqui for two years to maintain public order.

1921

President Coolidge strongly suggests the overthrow of *Guatemalan* President Carlos Herrera in the interests of United Fruit. The Guatemalans comply.

1925

U.S. Army troops occupy *Panama* City to break a rent strike and keep order.

1926

Marines, who had been out of *Nicaragua* for less than a year, occupy the country again, to settle a volatile political situation. Secretary of State Kellogg describes a "Nicaraguan-Mexican-Soviet" conspiracy to inspire a "Mexican-Bolshevist hegemony" within striking distance of the Canal.

"That intervention is not now, never was, and never will be a set policy of the United States is one of the most important facts President-elect Hoover has made clear."
—New York Times, 1928

1929

The United States establishes a military academy in *Nicaragua* to train a National Guard as the country's army. Similar forces are trained in Haiti and the Dominican Republic.

"There is no room for any outside influence other than ours in this region. We could not tolerate such a thing without incurring grave risks ... Until now Central America has always understood that governments which we recognize and support stay in power, while those which we do not recognize and support fall. Nicaragua has become a test case. It is difficult to see how we can afford to be defeated."
—Undersecretary of State Robert Olds

1930

Rafael Leonidas Trujillo emerges from the U.S.-trained National Guard to become dictator of the *Dominican Republic*.

1932

The United States rushes warships to *El Salvador* in response to a communist-led uprising. However, President Martínez prefers to put down the rebellion with his own forces, killing over eight thousand people (the rebels had killed about one hundred).

1933
President Roosevelt announces the Good Neighbor policy.

1933
Unable to suppress the guerrilla warfare of General Augusto César Sandino, Marines finally leave *Nicaragua*. Anastasio Somoza García becomes the first Nicaraguan commander of the National Guard.
"The Nicaraguans are better fighters than the Haitians, being of Indian blood, and as warriors similar to the aborigines who resisted the advance of civilization in this country."
—New York Times *correspondent Harold Denny*

1933
Roosevelt sends warships to Cuba to intimidate Gerardo Machado y Morales, who is massacring the people to put down nationwide strikes and riots. Machado resigns. The first provisional government lasts only seventeen days; the second Roosevelt finds too left-wing and refuses to recognize. A pro-Machado counter-coup is put down by Fulgencio Batista, who with Roosevelt's blessing becomes Cuba's new strongman.

1934
Platt Amendment repealed.

1934
Sandino assassinated by agents of Somoza, with U.S. approval. Somoza assumes the presidency of *Nicaragua* two years later. To block his ascent, Secretary of State Cordell Hull explains, would be to intervene in the internal affairs of Nicaragua.

1936
U.S. relinquishes rights to unilateral intervention in *Panama*.

1941
Ricardo Adolfo de la Guardia deposes *Panamanian* president Arias in a military coup—after first clearing it with the U.S. ambassador.

"It was 'a great relief' to us, because Arias had been very troublesome and very pro-Nazi."
—Secretary of War Henry Stimson

1943

The editor of the *Honduran* opposition paper *El Cronista* is summoned to the U.S. embassy and told that criticism of the dictator Tiburcio Carías Andino is damaging to the war effort. Shortly afterward, the paper is shut down by the government.

1944

The dictator Maximiliano Hernández Martínez of *El Salvador* is ousted by a revolution; the interim government is overthrown five months later by the dictator's former chief of police. The immediate recognition of the new dictator by the United States does much to tarnish Roosevelt's Good Neighbor policy in the eyes of Latin Americans.

1946

U.S. Army *School of the Americas* opens in *Panama* as a hemisphere-wide military academy. Its linchpin is the doctrine of National Security, by which the chief threat to a nation is internal subversion; this will be the guiding principle behind dictatorships in Brazil, Argentina, Uruguay, Chile, Central America, and elsewhere.

1948

José Figueres Ferrer wins a short civil war to become President of *Costa Rica*. Figueres is supported by the United States, which has informed San José that its forces in the Panama Canal are ready to come to the capital to end "communist control" of Costa Rica.

1954

Jacobo Arbenz Guzmán, elected president of *Guatemala*, introduces land reform and seizes some idle lands of United Fruit— proposing to pay for them the value United Fruit claimed on its tax returns. The CIA organizes a small force to overthrow him and begins training it in Honduras. When Arbenz naively asks for U.S. military help to meet this threat, he is refused; when he buys arms from Czechoslovakia it only proves he's a Red.

Guatemala is *"openly and diligently toiling to create a Communist state in Central America ... only two hours' bombing time from the Panama Canal."*
—*Life*

The CIA broadcasts reports detailing the imaginary advance of the "rebel army," and provides planes to strafe the capital. The army refuses to defend Arbenz, who resigns. The dictator handpicked by the United States, Carlos Castillo Armas, outlaws political parties, reduces the franchise, and establishes the death penalty for strikers, as well as undoing Arbenz's land reform. Over one hundred thousand citizens are killed in the next thirty years of military rule.

"This is the first instance in history where a Communist government has been replaced by a free one."
—Richard Nixon

1957

Eisenhower establishes the Office of Public Safety to train Latin American police forces.

1959

Fidel Castro takes power in *Cuba*. Several months earlier he had undertaken a triumphal tour through the United States which included a CIA briefing on the Red menace.

"Castro's continued tawdry little melodrama of invasion."
—Time, on Castro's warnings of an imminent U.S. invasion

1960

Eisenhower authorizes covert actions to get rid of Castro. Among other things, the CIA tries assassinating him with exploding cigars and poisoned milkshakes. Other covert actions against *Cuba* include burning sugar fields, blowing up boats in Cuban harbors, and sabotaging industrial equipment.

1960

The *Canal Zone* becomes the focus of U.S. counterinsurgency training.

1960

A new junta in *El Salvador* promises free elections; Eisenhower, fearing leftist tendencies, withholds recognition. A more attractive right-wing counter-coup comes along in three months.
"Governments of the civil-military type of El Salvador are the most effective in containing communist penetration in Latin America."
—John F. Kennedy, after the coup

1960

Guatemalan officers attempt to overthrow the regime of Presidente Fuentes; Eisenhower stations warships and two thousand Marines offshore while Fuentes puts down the revolt. (Another source says that the United States provided air support for Fuentes.)

1960s

U.S. Green Berets train *Guatemalan* army in counterinsurgency techniques. Guatemalan efforts against its insurgents include aerial bombing, scorched-earth assaults on towns suspected of aiding the rebels, and death squads, which killed twenty thousand people between 1966 and 1976. U.S. Army Col. John Webber claims that it was at his instigation that "the technique of counter-terror had been implemented by the army."
"If it is necessary to turn the country into a cemetery in order to pacify it, I will not hesitate to do so."
—President Carlos Arana Osorio

1961

The United States organizes a force of 1400 anti-Castro *Cubans* and ships it to the Bahía de los Cochinos. Castro's army routs it.

1961
CIA-backed coup overthrows elected president J. M. Velasco Ibarra of *Ecuador*, who has been too friendly with Cuba.

1962
CIA engages in campaign in *Brazil* to keep João Goulart from achieving control of Congress.

1963
CIA-backed coup overthrows elected social democrat Juan Bosch in the *Dominican Republic*.

1963
A far-right-wing coup in *Guatemala*, apparently U.S.-supported, forestalls elections in which "extreme leftist" Juan José Arévalo was favored to win.
"It is difficult to develop stable and democratic government [in Guatemala], because so many of the nation's Indians are illiterate and superstitious."
—*School textbook, 1964*

1964
João Goulart of **Brazil** proposes agrarian reform, nationalization of oil. Ousted by U.S.-supported military coup.

1964
The free market in *Nicaragua*:
The Somoza family controls *"about one-tenth of the cultivable land in Nicaragua, and just about everything else worth owning, the country's only airline, one television station, a newspaper, a cement plant, textile mill, several sugar refineries, half-a-dozen breweries and distilleries, and a Mercedes-Benz agency."*
—*Life World Library*

1965
A coup in the *Dominican Republic* attempts to restore Bosch's government. The United States invades and occupies the

country to stop this "Communist rebellion" with the help of the dictators of Brazil, Paraguay, Honduras, and Nicaragua.
"Representative democracy cannot work in a country such as the Dominican Republic," Bosch declares later. Now why would he say that?

1966

The United States sends arms, advisors, and Green Berets to *Guatemala* to implement a counterinsurgency campaign.
"To eliminate a few hundred guerrillas, the government killed perhaps 10,000 Guatemalan peasants."
—*U.S. State Department report on the program*

1967

A team of Green Berets is sent to *Bolivia* to help find and assassinate Che Guevara.

1968

Gen. José Alberto Medrano, who is on the payroll of the CIA, organizes the ORDEN paramilitary force, considered the precursor of *El Salvador's* death squads.

1970

In this year (just as an example), U.S. investments in Latin America earn $1.3 billion, while new investments total $302 million.

1970

Salvador Allende Gossens is elected in *Chile*. He suspends foreign loans and nationalizes foreign companies. With regards to the phone system, he pays ITT the company's minimized valuation for tax purposes. The CIA provides covert financial support for Allende's opponents both during and after his election.

1972

The United States stands by as the military in *El Salvador* suspends an election which centrist José Napoleón Duarte was favored to win. (Compare with the emphasis placed on the 1982 elections.)

1973

U.S.-supported military coup kills Allende and brings Augusto Pinochet Ugarte to power. Pinochet imprisons well over a hundred thousand *Chileans* (torture and rape are the usual methods of interrogation), terminates civil liberties, abolishes unions, extends the work week to forty-eight hours, and reverses Allende's land reforms.

1973

Military takes power in *Uruguay*, supported by the United States. The subsequent repression reportedly features the world's highest percentage of the population imprisoned for political reasons.

1974

The Office of Public Safety is abolished when it is revealed that police are being taught torture techniques.

1976

Election of Jimmy Carter leads to a new emphasis on human rights in Central America. Carter cuts off aid to the *Guatemalan* military (or tries to; some slips through) and reduces aid to *El Salvador*.

1979

Ratification of the Panama Canal treaty which is to return the Canal to *Panama* by 1999.
"Once again, Uncle Sam put his tail between his legs and crept away rather than face trouble."
—Ronald Reagan

1980

A right-wing junta takes over in *El Salvador*. The United States begins massively supporting El Salvador, assisting the military in its fight against FMLN guerrillas. Death squads proliferate,

Archbishop Romero is assassinated by right-wing terrorists, and thirty-five thousand civilians are killed in 1978–81. The rape and murder of four U.S. churchwomen results in the suspension of U.S. military aid for one month. The United States demands that the junta undertake land reform; however, within three years, the reform program is halted by the oligarchy.
"The Soviet Union underlies all the unrest that is going on." — Ronald Reagan

1980

Seeking a stable base for its actions in El Salvador and Nicaragua, the United States tells the *Honduran* military to clean up its act and hold elections. The United States starts pouring in $100 million of aid a year and basing the *contras* on Honduran territory. Death squads are also active in Honduras, and the *contras* tend to act as a state within a state.

1981

The CIA steps in to organize the *contras* in *Nicaragua* who started the previous year as a group of sixty ex-National Guardsmen; by 1985, there are about twelve thousand of them. Forty-six of the forty-eight top military leaders are ex-Guardsmen. The United States also sets up an economic embargo of Nicaragua and pressures the IMF and the World Bank to limit or halt loans to Nicaragua.

1981

Gen. Torrijos of *Panama* is killed in a plane crash. There is a suspicion of CIA involvement due to Torrijos's nationalism and friendly relations with Cuba.

1982

A coup brings Gen. Efraín Ríos Montt to power in *Guatemala* and gives the Reagan administration the opportunity to increase military aid. Ríos Montt's evangelical beliefs do not prevent him from accelerating the counterinsurgency campaign.

1983

Another coup in *Guatemala* replaces Ríos Montt. The new president, Oscar Mejía Víctores, was trained by the United States and seems to have cleared his coup beforehand with U.S. authorities.

1983

U.S. troops take over tiny *Granada*. Rather oddly, the United States intervenes shortly after a coup has overthrown the previous socialist leader. One of the justifications for the action is the building of a new airport with Cuban help, which Granada claimed was for tourism and Reagan argued was for Soviet use. Later the United States announced plans to finish the airport ... to develop tourism.

1983

Boland Amendment prohibits the CIA and Defense Department from spending money to overthrow the government of *Nicaragua*—a law the Reagan administration cheerfully violates.

1984

The CIA mines three *Nicaraguan* harbors. Nicaragua takes this action to the World Court, which brings an $18 billion judgment against the United States. The United States refuses to recognize the Court's jurisdiction over the case.

1984

The United States spends $10 million to orchestrate elections in *El Salvador*—which is something of a farce as left-wing parties are under heavy repression, and the military has already declared that it will not answer to the elected president.

1989

The United States invades *Panama* to dislodge CIA-boy-gone-wrong Manuel Noriega, an event that marks the favorite excuse of the United States for intervention evolving from communism to drugs.

1996
The United States battles global communism by extending most-favored-nation trading status to China and tightening the trade embargo on Castro's *Cuba*.

WHERE TO GO FOR MORE INFORMATION

- Black, George. *The Good Neighbor*. Pantheon Books, New York: 1988. Highly recommended. An often amusing history of U.S. attitudes toward its southern neighbors.
- Burns, E. Bradford. *Latin America: A concise interpretive history*. 4th ed. Prentice-Hall, Englewood Cliffs: 1986. Not only what the U.S. does to Latin America, but what Europe and the Latin Americans do to Latin America.
- Chomsky, Noam. *Year 501: The Conquest Continues*. South End Press, Boston: 1993. Packed with documentation.
- Galeano, Eduardo. *Century of the Wind* and *Faces & Masks*. Pantheon Books, New York: 1988. (Originally published as *Memoria del fuego II, III: El siglo del viento, Las caras y las mascaras*.) Vignettes from history, from a master Latin American novelist. As history, take it with a grain of salt.
- Gleijeses, Piero. *Shattered Hope: The Guatemalan Revolution and the United States, 1944-1954*. Princeton, Princeton NJ: 1991. The definitive study of the Arévalo/Arbenz administrations and the U.S. coup.
- Kwitny, Jonathan. *Endless Enemies: The Making of an Unfriendly World*. Congdon & Weed, New York: 1984. By a former *Wall Street Journal* reporter.

OTHER PUBLICATIONS BY DARIO LISIERO

1. **Dario Lisiero**, *People Ideology, People Theology*, Exposition Press, New York 1980.

2. **Dario Lisiero**, *My First Life*, Trafford, Victoria (Canada) 2004.

3. **Dario Lisiero**, *Angelica*, Lulu, New York 2006

4. **Dario Lisiero**, *José Benito Lamas, I. Reconstrucción histórica del gobierno eclesiástico en 1852-1857*, Editorial Dunken, Buenos Aires 2003.

5. **Dario Lisiero**, *José Benito Lamas, II. Relectura del pensamiento y de la acción de José Benito Lamas*, Editorial Dunken, Buenos Aires 2004.

6. **Dario Lisiero**, *Uruguayana*, Lulu, New York 2006.

7. **Dario Lisiero**, *El Vicario Apostólico Jacinto Vera, Lustro Definitorio en la Historia del Uruguay, Primera Parte*, Lulu, New York 2006.

8. **Dario Lisiero**, *El Vicario Apostólico Jacinto Vera, Lustro Difinitorio en la Historia del Uruguay, Segunda Parte*, Lulu, New York 2006.

9. **Dario Lisiero**, *El Vicario de Montevideo*, Lulu, New York 2007.

10. **Dario Lisiero**, *Justice Unfinished*, Lulu: New York, 2008.

www.ingramcontent.com/pod-product-compliance
Lightning Source LLC
Chambersburg PA
CBHW032250150426
43195CB00008BA/397